Acknowledgements

Compiled by Peter and Cynthia Empson
With special thanks to Evelyne Richir, of the International Council of Hi Kidz Foundation in Switzerland, for many of the games.
Design and typesetting by Paul Stockley
Graphics by Matthew Slater
Proofreading by Lorna Stanley

2nd Edition

ISBN: 1-897987-28-5

Printed and bound in India by OM Authentic Media, P.O. Box 2014, Secunderabad – 500 003 email: printing@ombooks.org

URBAN SAINTS

For over 100 years Urban Saints has been committed to helping children and young people reach their God-given potential and live lives of faith, hope and love through following the words and actions of Jesus Christ.

Urban Saints is primarily involved in work in the UK and Ireland with tens of thousands of children and young people attending local groups with a Christian emphasis.

In addition, a significant and growing proportion of the work occurs within partnerships in many other countries around the world, through leadership training and support.

For more information, please contact us at:

Urban Saints Support Centre, Kestin House, 45 Crescent Road, Luton, Bedfordshire, LU2 0AH, UK.

Tel. +44 (0) 1582 589850
Fax. +44 (0) 1582 721702

UK Registered Charity No. 223798

www.urbansaints.org email@urbansaints.org

Contents

Welcome to Easy Games!

Are you ever at a loss for games ideas? Never again!

This book is written to help you play games with children and young people, especially when you don't have much equipment.

How to Use this Book

The first time you pick up this book, you need to read through this Getting Ready section to familiarise yourself with the different types of games, how to make games equipment, and so on.

Once you have done this, you just need a few simple steps to get you going...

Choose Some Games

- consider the children's age and ability,
- include different types of games for variety, and
- select a few extra, in case you need to fill in time.

Prepare Any Equipment

- make enough batons and balls for the number of teams and players,
- get any extra items needed (balloons, buckets, pencils, paper and such), and
- find a safe space to play.

Explain Clear Instructions

- the name of the game,
- the objective,
- rules of how to play,
- any penalty for cheating, and
- how the winner is determined.

Play!

- have a trial run if necessary,
- make sure all players get a turn, and
- stop before anyone gets bored!

Have fun!

Five Types of Easy Game

In this book we have grouped the games into five types: all together, in a circle, in groups, relay races, and two teams.

All Together

These are games in which everybody can participate together. There are no teams. In some of these games players are eliminated leaving one or two winners. Other games have no winners, just the fun of playing!

This section includes 'icebreaker' games, which are good for introducing leaders and children to each other, especially if members are new.

In a Circle

Circle games are those games where you begin with all players in a circle. Depending on the game they may be facing outwards or inwards, sitting down or standing up.

Forming a Circle

To organise children for circle games (especially young children), it helps to ask them to form a circle by holding hands. If the circle is too small, ask them to drop their hands and take a step backwards. If they are too far apart, ask them to take a step closer.

Playing in Circles

The players need to understand that even when they are 'out', they are not to leave the circle until the game is over (unless specifically directed), as this frequently makes it impossible for the remaining players to continue the game!

In Groups

Most of the group games are played with children in teams each seated in a semi–

circle in a different corner of the playing area.

It is a good idea to divide the children into teams first (see: Forming Teams). the balance of players in each group may vary.

Relay Races

Relays are made up of two or more teams of the same number of players, playing in parallel. (For example four teams of ten players each.)

Each player on the team takes their turn in the activity until all have played.

Normally the teams need to line up in a straight line to start and finish the game.

Two Teams

These games involve two teams only playing in opposition against each other, with the leader keeping the score.

Forming Teams

To avoid ending up with the little children on one team and the bigger young people on the other, the following method might help.

Ask the children to stand in a straight line, with the smallest at one end and the tallest at the other end. Decide how many teams you need. Then starting at one end of the line, count the children off in turn, A, B, A, B, A, B, etc. for two teams, or A, B, C, A, B, C, etc. for three teams, for example.

With them still in a line, ask all the A team players to raise their hands. Tell them to go into one corner, or one line (depending on the game). Then ask the B team to raise their hands, and so on. This way you will divide the teams evenly and fairly.

Playing with Teams

In some Two Team games, not all the players play at once. Only one or two from each team play at a time.

Before the game starts, and while they are in their teams, give each player a number starting with the smallest player, and ending with the tallest (1, 2, 3, 4, 5, etc.). This way you know how many are in each team and that all the teams have an equal number of players.

List the numbers of the team players on a piece of paper. As you call out the numbers of the players to have their turn, cross out their numbers on the list, to remember who has played. Keep playing by calling the others until all the children have had a turn.

It is no fun for a child to be left out, particularly if others have had more than one turn playing the game. This method ensures everyone has a fair turn!

Additional Games

Some games are sub-titled as Bible Games or as Icebreakers.

Using Games with the Bible

In each category you will find some games which help to bring the Bible to life.

When using games to tell a Bible story or to teach memory verses, it is important to ensure that the children understand the story itself and the context of it. Otherwise, you may get them confused, thinking (for example) that Joseph, with his coloured coat is the same person as the husband of Mary, mother of Jesus!

Sometimes it is helpful to stop the game before you reach the end of the story, and tell the children something like:

> 'We will stop the game now, but I want you to listen carefully while I finish the story because...'

Now you have their full attention as you get to the point of the story.

Do not assume that the children will know the storyline of the Bible, or understand theological words, like 'sin' or 'baptism' etc.

So, when you want them to learn a Bible verse, it is vital you: explain how it fits into a book of the Bible (the context), what the verse means (including any difficult words) and how the verse can help them. Only then will it be a useful thing to learn.

If you have very young children, make sure the Bible verse is short — just a few words. It can be part of a verse. For instance, instead of expecting them to learn all of John 8:12, they could learn:

Jesus said, 'I am the light of the world'.

An older child would have no trouble learning all of the verse, so make sure you keep in mind the children's abilities.

Using Games as Icebreakers

Icebreakers are games which are good to play at the beginning of a club, especially when there are new children present. These games are designed to help children enjoy participating and get to know each other.

Equipment for Games

You don't need expensive equipment to play games. Many games in this book need no equipment at all.

Any items you might need you will find readily available very cheaply or at no cost.

Here we explain how you can make the most common basic games equipment using discarded oddments such as old newspaper, platic bags, and string.

Rope Ring

A few games require a ring or quoit. You can make a good ring out of thin rope. You will need about five to seven metres of it.

a) fold a loop in the head of the rope then make a circle bigger than your fist

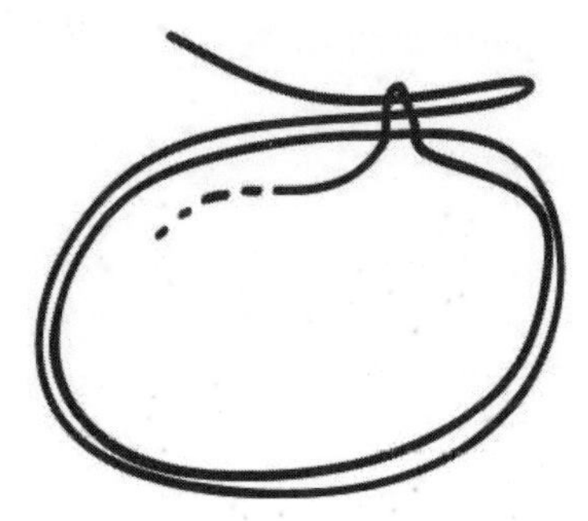

b) add three or four more turns to the circle then start winding tightly around the core strands leaving the loop free

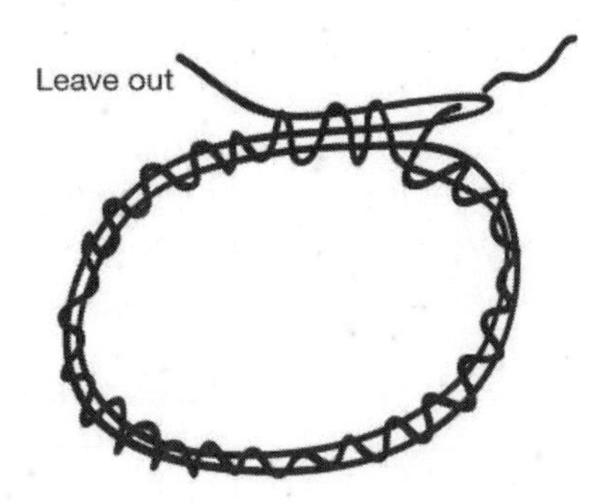

c) after several windings leave loose end free and keep winding until you have fully covered the core strands

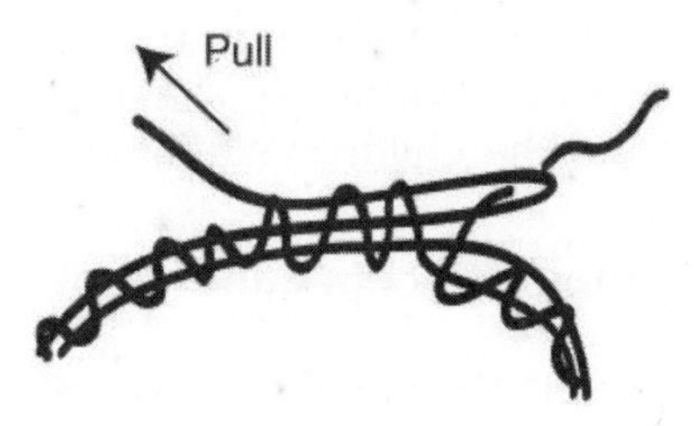

d) put loose tail end through the head loop then pull the loop into the core of the ring and cut off loose ends

If rope is unavailable, you can form a ring from newspaper and tape.

Take a couple of sheets of newspaper and roll them up like a baton. Then bend the ends round so that they overlap each other. Tape the join, then tape all the way round the ring for strength.

Paper or Plastic Ball

Any sheets of old newspaper or plastics will serve to make some balls. String or tape is needed to stop them coming apart!

Now, just follow these simple instructions...

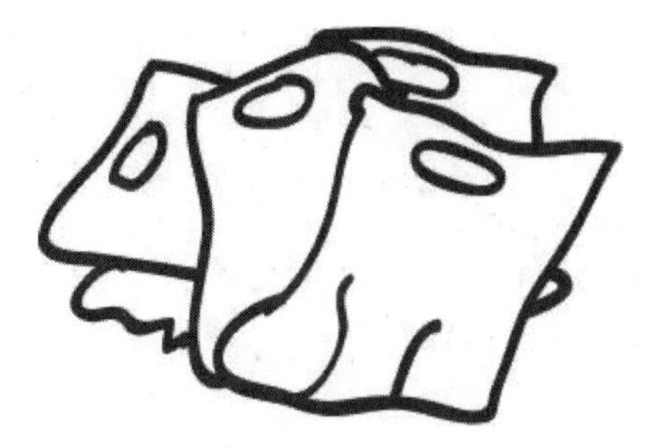

use newspaper or plastic bags

squeeze them into a ball

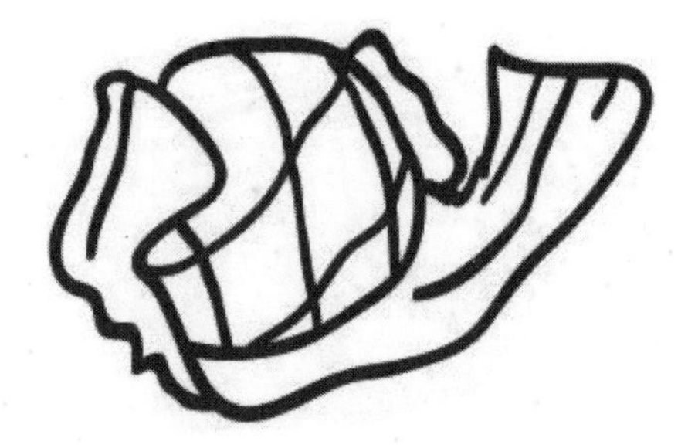

wrap more layers until size required

tie tightly with fine string or parcel tape

Voilá! That wasn't difficult. Now to hit the ball you need some batons...

Paper Baton

Newspaper is needed to make batons for the games. Again, you will need string or tape to hold them together.

three newspapers

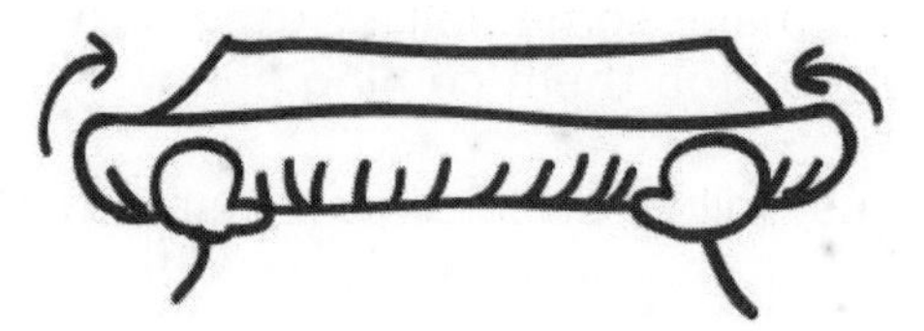

roll very tightly

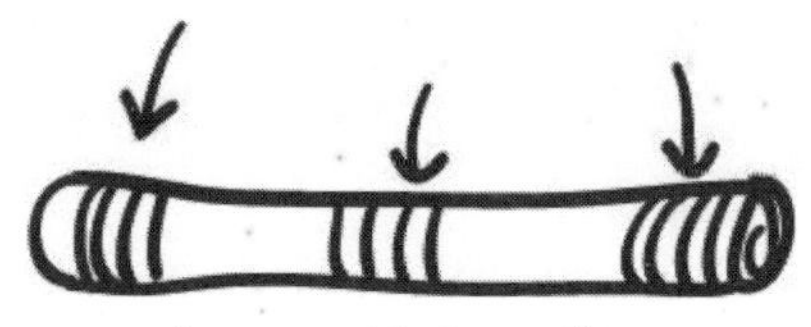

tape or tie together

Make a few more, and you will be fully equipped for most of the games.

Other Items

We recommend you make six newspaper batons, and four balls. With more than four teams you will need more batons and balls.

In addition, for some games you may need some of the following items.

- sheets of plain paper
- pens or pencils
- balloons
- 7 small items (stones or shells)
- 1 pole or stick
- 1 ring or quoit

Anything you require is listed at the beginning of the game instructions.

You may also find a whistle comes in useful!

Tips and Hints

- Make sure you have any equipment you need before you start.
- Make sure you have a safe space in which to play.
- Make sure you understand the game completely before you introduce it.
- Ensure you have the children's attention and quiet before you start explaining. Don't try to talk or shout over the noise being made.
- Know the rules and explain clearly to the children or young people.
- Know how to quickly get the children into the formation you want.
- If it is a new game, it may help if some leaders demonstrate how to play.
- It may help to have a trial run first, rather than lengthy explanations.
- Referee fairly, be aware of what is going on and keep control at all times.

- If someone does something disruptive in a game you can ask in a friendly way for that person to stand out of the game for half a minute.
- If you have problems with control, give extra points for good behaviour.
- Make sure that your leaders join in the games, and ensure they keep the rules!
- In games where some players are eliminated, make sure those who are 'out' can watch or have something to do, so they don't get restless.
- Don't keep playing a game until players get bored. Stop while still enjoying it. Then they will want to play next time.
- Remember to cater for all children you may have of different abilities.
- Remember that God is happy to see young people having a fun time.
- Be enthusiastic!

And by the way, when you are tired of these games, go and invent some of your own!

Easy Index

All Together

Game	need no equip	space to play	age range	number players	time to play	number leaders	energy level	page number
Balloon Burst		M	bcd	30	10	2	***	27
Cat and Mouse	x	M	bc	10–40	5	1	***	29
Catch Out	x	L	b	20–40	5	1	***	31
Chain Chase	x	L	bc	10–40	5–10	1	****	33
Change Direction	x	L	b	18–38	5	1	**	35
Clap Hands		any	abcd	any	5	1	*	37
Detective	x	any	bcd	20–60	10	2	*	39
Did You Know?		any	bcd	10+	10–15	1–2	*	41
Elimination		S	bc	10+	5	1	*	43
Grandma's Keys		L	bcd	10–20	10	2	*	45
Hunt the Object		M	a	5–10	10	2	**	47
Islands		L	abcd	any	5	2	****	49
I Spy	x	S	a	5–10	5–10	1–2	**	51
Jerusalem Jericho	x	S	bc	5–20	5	1	**	53
Knee Trip		L	bcd	10+	5–10	2	****	55
Musical Chairs		M	abcd	10+	10	2	**	57
Poison		L	b	1–2	5–10	1	**	59
Portraits	x	M	bcd	10–20	10–15	2	*	61
Statues		M	bc	10–40	5–10	1–2	*	63

In a Circle

In Groups

Relay Races

Game	need no equip	space to play	age range	number players	time to play	number leaders	energy level	page number
Ball Roll		L	bc		5	2	***	151
Bible Footsteps		L	b	36	5	2	**	153
Bible Text Relay		L	bc	12+	10	2+	*	155
Bible Quiz		M	abc	12+	5–10	2	*	157
Car Race		L	bcd	40	5	2	***	159
Chain Run		L	bcd	10–40	5	1	***	161
Chariots		L	bcd	60	5	2	****	163
Cross the River		L	bcd	10–24	10–15	1–2	***	165
Donkey's Tail		M	ab	16–20	10	3–4	*	167
Fun Relay		L	bcd	12+	5	2	*	169
Mass Exhaustion		L	bcd	10–40	5	2	****	171
Right Order	x	L	cd	10–30	5–15	2	**	173
Story Relay	x	L	abc	12–30	10	2	*	175
Team Catch		M	b	40	5	2	***	177
Telephone Chain	x	M	bcd	12–30	5	2+	*	179
Throw Ball		L	bc	10–40	5	2	**	181
Tunnel Ball		L	bc	10–40	5	2	***	183
Under Over		?	bcd	10–40	5	2	***	185
Water Relay		L	bcd	10–30	10	2–3	***	187

Two Teams

Game	need no equip	space to play	age range	number players	time to play	number leaders	energy level	page number
Balloon Smash		M	ab	10–20	10	1	**	191
Bash Away		M	bc	10–30	5–10	1	***	193
Binball		L	bcd	20–40	10–15	2	****	195
Cap Snatch		M	bcd	10–20	10	2	**	197
Chair Balloon Bash		L	bcd	40	10	4	**	199
Crocker		L	bcd	20–50	30	3	****	201
Guess What?		S	bcd	30	10	1	*	203
Hit the Bottle		L	bcd	10–40	10–20	3	****	205
Hit the Tin		L	bcd	16–30	10	2	****	207
Kabadi		L	bcd	12	10	2	****	209
Ladder Balloons		M	bc	16–20	5–10	1	***	211
Not Funny	x	M	abc	12–40	5–10	1	**	213
Noughts and Crosses		M	bcd	20	10	2	**	215
Paper Fight		M	bcd	20	5	2	***	217
Ringer		L	bcd	10–40	15–30	3	****	219
Round the Circle		L	bcd	20–40	10	2	***	221
Snake's Tail		L	bcd	10–40	10	2	****	223
Snatch It		M	bcd	10–30	10	2	*	225
Sound Barrier	x	M	bc	16–24	10	1	**	227
Waterballoon		L	bcd	4+	5	1	**	229
Water Volleyballoon		L	bcd	12–30	10	2	***	231

Key to the Index Columns

needs no equipment
only players and some space required!

space to play
L = large,
M = medium,
S = small,
or 'any'.

age range
approximately:
a = 3–5 years,
b = 6–10 years,
c = 11–14 years,
d = 15–18 years.

number of players
about how many players needed.

time to play
how many minutes required.

energy level
the more stars, the more energy!

Symbols for Games Diagrams

Some games in the sections that follow use a diagram to indicate how to play. The following symbols are used:

leader 

player 

opponent 

direction of play 

Any other items are noted in the diagrams.

All Together

These are games in which everybody can participate together. There are no teams. In some of these games players are eliminated leaving one or two winners. Other games have no winners, just the fun of playing!

Balloon Burst

space	medium
age	8 to 18
number	30
time	10 minutes
leaders	2

YOU WILL NEED

- balloons
- woollen thread
- scissors

FORMATION

Children scattered round the area with a balloon tied loosely to their ankles.

HOW TO PLAY

Take a balloon for each child and with a one metre woollen cord attach it to their ankle. At the start everyone tries to stamp on another child's balloon to burst it. If their balloon is burst they have to sit out of the game and cannot burst any one else's balloon.

Be careful you don't tie the wool tight around the ankle or it may cut into the skin. You may also need some spare balloons!

WINNER

The last person to have their balloon intact.

VARIATIONS

1. Run the game with four teams with each team having a different colour balloon.
2. One or two children come out from each team to do battle! Keep points for the winning teams.

LEARNING POINT

We need to be watching out for others who want to spoil our life.

Cat and Mouse

space	medium
age	8 to 18
number	10 to 40
time	5 minutes
leaders	1

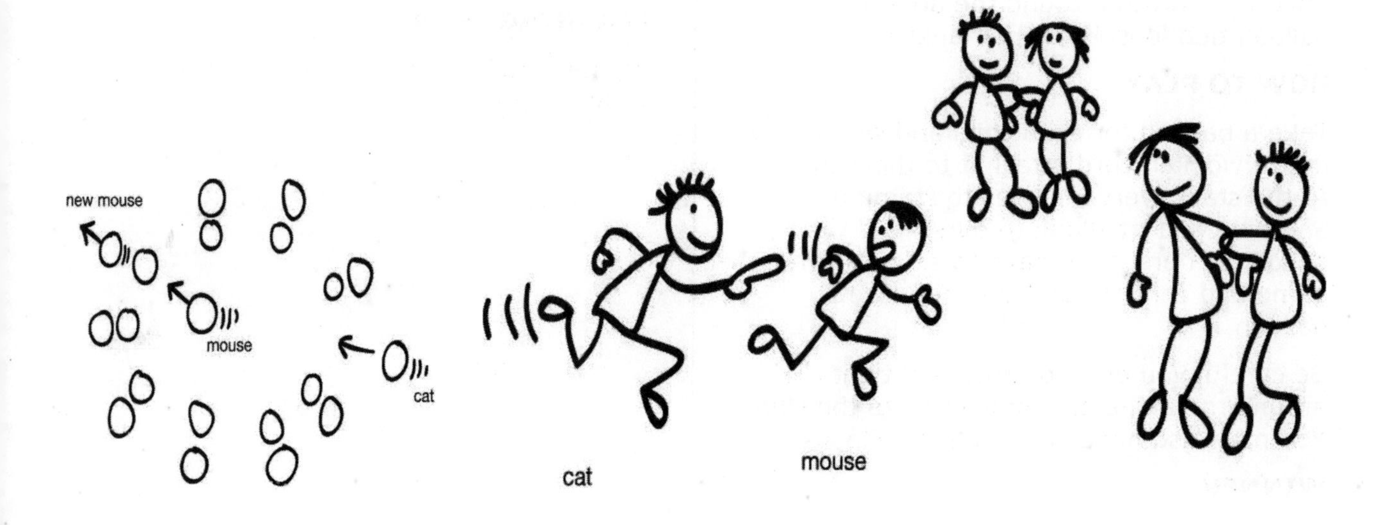

YOU WILL NEED

Nothing.

FORMATION

Scattered groups of two, linked arm in arm.

HOW TO PLAY

The groups of two's are scattered about the hall (arm in arm). There are two others — a cat and a mouse. The cat has to chase the mouse and if touched the mouse becomes the cat and chases the other. For the mouse to escape it has to link arms with one of the couples. When this happens the child at the other end becomes the mouse and has to move off very quickly, and the game continues. (If some people are not getting a chance to be the mouse, then have them raise their hands so the mouse knows where to go.)

WINNER

No real winner!

VARIATION

If people do not like linking arms ask the pairs to stand in a circle facing in but with one standing behind the other. When the mouse wants a rest they just stand in front of one of the pairs, releasing the person at the back who now becomes the mouse.

LEARNING POINT

There is always a way of escape if we want to take it.

Catch Out

space	large
age	5 to 10
number	20 to 40
time	5 minutes
leaders	1

YOU WILL NEED

Nothing.

FORMATION

Children in an area which is clearly marked out with chairs, or a marked area on the floor, about 5 metres square.

HOW TO PLAY

You need a catcher who could be a leader or a child. With the children on one side of the hall blow the whistle and the children have to cross to the other side without being caught by the catcher. When there, they wait for the whistle to cross back again. Those caught join the catcher in the middle and help to catch others. If children hold back for a long time before trying to cross you could add a rule that the last one to leave is also out.

WINNER

Is the last one in.

LEARNING POINT

Some people are always trying to catch others out and make them copy their bad behaviour.

Chain Chase

space	large
age	8 to 14
number	10 to 40
time	5 to 10 minutes
leaders	1 to 2

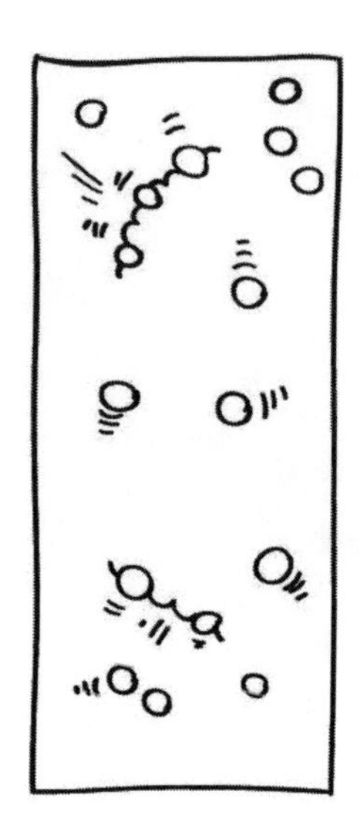

YOU WILL NEED

No equipment.

FORMATION

Anywhere in defined area.

HOW TO PLAY

The players are to scatter themselves all around the area.

One person is chosen to catch others. When he manages to touch a person, they hold hands and together, they try to catch another. Then they have three in the chain. When they catch the next person they split the 4 into two 2's. You cannot touch someone unless you are holding hands with your partner(s).

WINNER

Is the last person to be caught.

VARIATION

A more difficult adaptation is to let the chain keep growing instead of splitting up into two's. Great fun but sometimes difficult for the person on the end who sometimes has to travel at high speed!

Change Direction

(in rows or a grid)

space	large
age	8 to 14
number	18 to 38
time	5 minutes
leaders	1

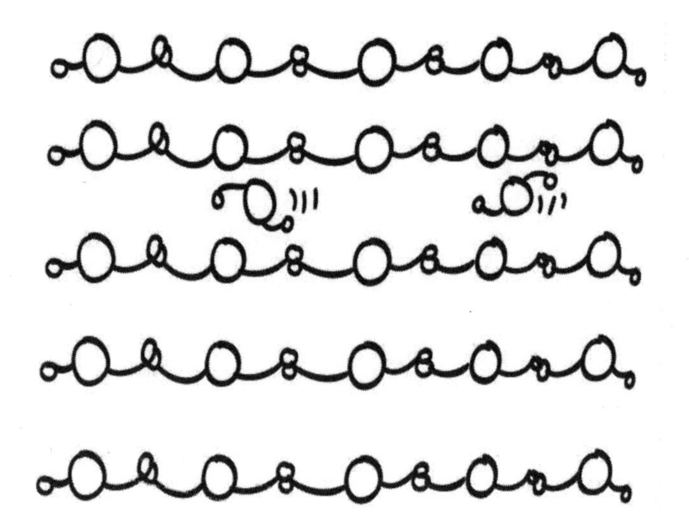

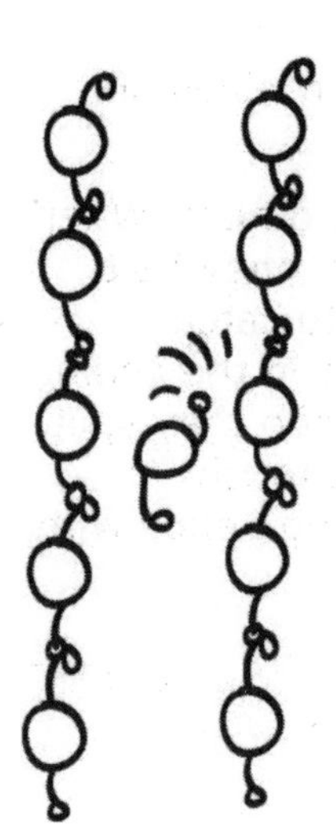

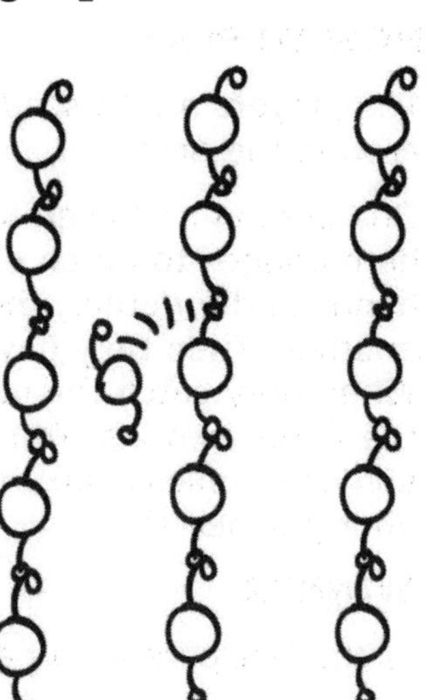

YOU WILL NEED

Nothing.

FORMATION

All but two (the 'cat' and the 'mouse') stand in four or five lines, with the same number of children in each line, facing the same way and all holding hands. The lines need to be close enough to let the children hold hands with the children in the lines on either side.

Important to practice the changes before the cat and mouse are let loose.

HOW TO PLAY

The cat runs after the mouse between the rows of children, (who form chains by holding hands). When the leader shouts 'change' or blows a whistle, those in the rows must let go the hands they are holding and turn to their right a quarter of a circle (at right angles) and hold hands with their new partners. There can be as many rotations as the leader calls for. Neither the cat nor mouse can go under or over, or break the joined hands.

WINNER

The cat, if it catches the mouse or the mouse, if it has not been caught after one minute!

VARIATION

Try playing with two cats and one mouse, but all blindfolded when they know the game well. The mouse must squeak loudly in reply to the cats' cries.

LEARNING POINT

In life, circumstances can change very quickly, but God doesn't change.

Clap Hands

space	small
age	5 to 18
number	any number
time	5 minutes
leaders	1

YOU WILL NEED

Maybe a chair.

FORMATION

Any formation will do so long as everyone can see you.

HOW TO PLAY

This is a very quick game which can be used to wake children up.

Stand so everyone can see you, maybe on a chair. Hold your left arm out straight but pointing down. Your right arm should be straight but pointing up to the ceiling. Tell everyone that they are to get ready to clap, when your hands pass each other. Practice this a few times. Now fool them all by suddenly stopping just before your hands cross over. Now eliminate those who clap when they should not. Also warn them that there should be no delay in people's reaction.

WINNER

Is the last person to be eliminated.

LEARNING POINT

To be alert.

Don't just do what everyone else does — make up your own mind.

Detective

space	any
age	8 to 18
number	20 to 60 (or more)
time	10 minutes
leaders	2

YOU WILL NEED

Nothing.

FORMATION

Can be played with a lot of children. Divide them down the middle of the area. Everyone stand.

HOW TO PLAY

You will need one detective, a child, to come out to the front from each side.

Tell the two detectives that they are to choose ONE person (a spy) from their side which the other detective has to identify.

When both detectives have chosen the one on their side (they whisper the name to the leader secretly). The spies themselves do not need to know they have been selected.

The game starts with each detective in turn asking the other such questions as: 'is the spy a boy'? The other detective can only say 'yes' or 'no'. If the answer is 'no' then all the boys on his team sit down. The next question may be, 'does the spy wear something red?' If the answer is 'no' then everyone wearing red sits down.

Carry on alternately, with the leader (who knows who the spies are) making sure the detective does not change his spy, until either only one is left or the detective guesses who the opposing team's spy is.

WINNER

Is the first detective to guess the opposing team's spy. Give a point to that team.

VARIATION

If some children are slow at sitting down and a leader has a water pistol, squirt those children with water.

LEARNING POINT

If you are a Christian can others notice that you are different from everyone else?

Did you Know?

(an Icebreaker)

space	any
age	8 or above
number	10 or more
time	10 to 15 minutes
leaders	1 to 2

Find a person who...	**Signature**
...plays a musical instrument	
...has two older brothers (or sisters)	
...is an uncle or aunt	
...has lived in another country (or town)	
...is the same age as you	

YOU WILL NEED

- a list of details, as in the example, enough for one sheet per person
- pen or pencil for each person

HOW TO PLAY

Give each person a list with typical descriptions of a number of leaders or children and a pen or pencil. They each must try and find someone in the room who fits one of the descriptions. That person must sign their name by it. They then go on to find someone else who fits another description on the list, and so on.

WINNER

Is the first to complete their list, signed by a different person for each item listed.

VARIATION

Who am I? (see Circle Games)

LEARNING POINT

People are different, have different tastes and each one is special.

Elimination

(a Bible verse game)

space	small
age	5 or above
number	10 or more
time	5 minutes
leaders	1

YOU WILL NEED

A Bible verse written out with each word on separate sheets of paper.

FORMATION

Those with the Bible words face the others or all stand in a circle.

HOW TO PLAY

Each word of the verse is given randomly to children — one each. They must hold them right way up and facing outwards. If not enough for all, the other children look at the words and advise them where to move to until the words are in their correct order and the verse can be read.

All need to read it aloud. Then have one child turn his or her verse over so it cannot be seen. Have all repeat the verse. Each time, turn over more words until they know the verse without any words showing.

WINNER

They all win when they have learnt the verse.

VARIATION

Verse on large sheet of paper. Keep repeating the verse. Each time one piece is cut away until nothing left.

OR

Tie string across the room like a washing line and peg the pieces of paper to it. Children take turns to move a word until they get them in the right order. Others can help them by calling instructions to them.

LEARNING POINTS

Be sure to explain the meaning of the verse and any words they don't understand. Ensure the children know how the verse can encourage them in their lives today.

Grandma's Keys

space	large
age	5 or above
number	10 to 20
time	10 minutes
leaders	2

YOU WILL NEED

- Bunch of keys, or similar
- Blindfold

FORMATION

The children line up at one end of the room, or in a semicircle with 'grandma' blindfolded at the other end, and is seated on a chair or on the floor. A leader must stay close behind 'grandma'. The keys, or an object, are put under her chair, or on the floor in front of her.

HOW TO PLAY

'Grandma' has to defend her keys. Everyone must be very quiet, including the leaders. When the game starts, the leader signals to four players who quietly creep forward to take the keys. If 'grandma' hears one of them, she (or he) points with her finger and if the leader sees a player is pointed at directly that player must stop and stand still while the others continue. Players may not run. More players can have a turn when the others have been stopped.

WINNER

Is the one who snatches the keys — or 'grandma' if she prevents everyone from doing so.

VARIATION

Older children can play the game with obstacles around the room, which they have to negotiate to reach 'grandma'.

'Grandma' can hold a paper baton and guard her keys with it, trying to hit anyone getting close enough to snatch the keys.

Hunt the Object

space	medium
age	3 to 6
number	5 to 10
time	5 to 10 minutes
leaders	2

YOU WILL NEED

Any small object the children are familiar with.

FORMATION

All sitting together on the floor.

HOW TO PLAY

The leader shows the children the object and explains it is going to be placed somewhere in the room, but NOT under anything or hidden out of sight. The children then hide their faces in their hands while the leader places the object somewhere.

The children are told they can start looking for it and the leader helps them by telling them whether they are near the object (hot), or not (cold). They may need to indicate whether they need to look high or low, behind or in front of something.

The child who finds it can then place it in a different place, while the others hide their faces again.

WINNER

Whoever finds the object first.

VARIATION

The children can leave the room while the object is being hidden

If there are more than ten children playing, let two children play at a time and the others watch and tell the players if they are 'hot' or 'cold'.

Islands

space large
age any age
number any number
time about 5 minutes
leaders 2

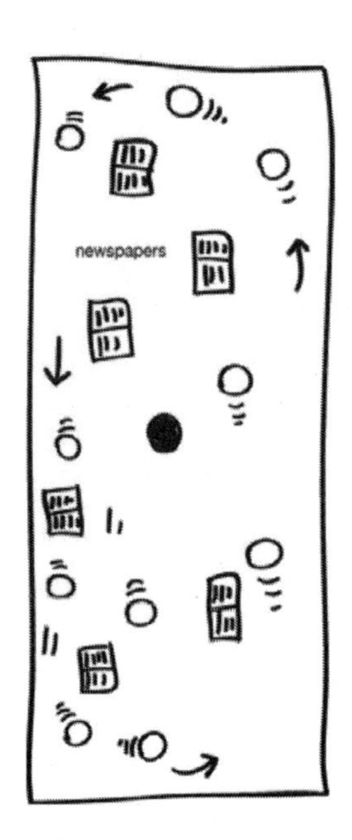

YOU WILL NEED

Sheets of newspaper or pieces of cardboard.

FORMATION

Before the start of the game, place sheets of newspaper (or cardboard) randomly around the central area of the floor.

Everyone moves in a circle round the outside of the 'islands' in the same direction.

HOW TO PLAY

Everyone must run round the outside of the paper islands. When the leader shouts 'storm', or blows a whistle, everyone has to stand on an island. Anyone with a part of their foot in the sea (on the floor) is out and sits down to watch the rest of the game. When the leader says 'storm over' or blows the whistle again they move outside of the islands and start running round again. This time a leader takes some of the islands away so more people have to crowd onto fewer islands.

WINNER

The last people standing on the last island!

VARIATION

If too many children let half of them make a circle around the paper islands holding hands so that the players move in a circle around them until the whistle is blown. Then those in the circle drop their hands and those playing have to find or share an island. Anyone who has the tiniest bit of foot in the sea is out and joins the circle. Afterwards, make sure all children change places so that the other half have their turn to play the game.

LEARNING POINTS

Children today need to know where they can go to be safe.

I Spy

space	small
age	3 or above
number	5 to 10
time	5 to 10 minutes
leaders	1 (2 for variation)

YOU WILL NEED

Nothing.

FORMATION

Everyone sitting down.

HOW TO PLAY

For small children who cannot read or write, categories need to be used.

The leader begins by saying, 'I spy with my little eye a T-shirt'. The children have to guess which T-shirt it is. Then the child who discovers it has his turn and tells the leader what he is choosing for the others to guess. The leader then helps him give the right clue. If the children know their colours, that can be one of the categories. For example 'I spy with my little eye, something red'.

WINNER

The winner is the child to discover the item.

VARIATIONS

- Older children who can read and write can use the alphabet for clues, by saying, 'I spy with my little eye, something beginning with the letter D.'
- The leader can ask the children to look at him or her, then leave the room and change his or her appearance in some way: such as putting shoes on the wrong feet, putting glasses on upside down, undoing a shirt button, or wearing a watch on the other wrist. The leader then returns to the room. The first child to notice the change wins. If in teams, give points and have a small prize.

LEARNING POINT

Seeking objects is fun, even though we may not always find them; but we can be sure of finding God, if we look for Him, as Jesus said, 'Seek and you will find.'

Jerusalem Jericho

space	small
age	8 to 14
number	5 to 20
time	5 minutes
leaders	1

YOU WILL NEED

No equipment.

FORMATION

The children stand where they can see the leader.

HOW TO PLAY

The leader will call out random words and the children must listen very carefully to what is said. If the name Jerusalem is mentioned the children are to bow at the waist. If Jericho is mentioned, they are to do nothing. Anyone who bows on hearing Jericho or does not bow for Jerusalem is 'out'. It is important that the children react immediately they hear the name and any hesitation or correction means they are out.

WINNER

The one who is last to be caught.

VARIATION

To trick the young people, the leader could bow himself at the wrong name. He could also use other names like Jeremiah or Jeremoth.

The names, Jerusalem, Jericho, even Jeremiah all have the same first syllable, so the children can't guess when you start to say the word, which one it is going to be and whether they have to bow, or not, so any other words with the same first syllable can be used.

LEARNING POINT

People will try to get us to bow down, or treat as very important, things that are quite wrong. We must listen and work out what is true and good before we say 'yes' to it.

Knee Trip

space	large
age	5 or above
number	more than 10
time	5 to 10 minutes
leaders	2

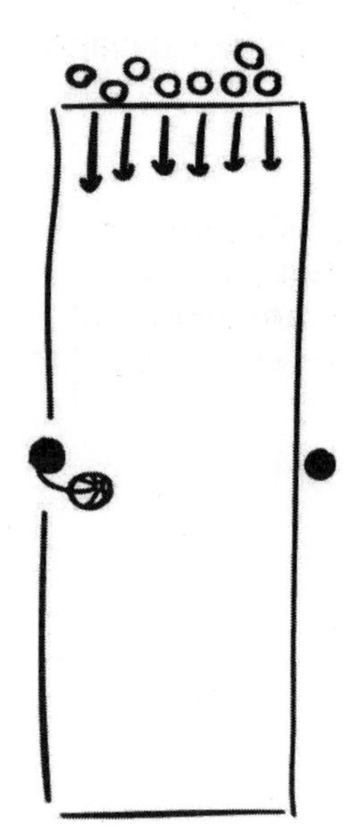

YOU WILL NEED

One or two large, soft balls, more if available.

FORMATION

Children stand at one end of the playing area; the leaders stand half-way along each side with the ball(s).

HOW TO PLAY

The idea is that when the leader says 'go' everyone has to run from one end of the hall to the other without being touched by the ball which will be thrown by the leaders. If the person is hit at or below the knee they are 'dead' and have to go to the side where they can help catch others out. Bring a second ball into play after a few minutes.

WINNER

The winner is the last person left in.

VARIATION

Use 4 or 5 balls, which adds to the fun.

Those who are 'out' stand exactly where they are when hit. They then become an obstacle for those who are still 'in' and can also be given one of the balls to throw.

Musical Chairs

space medium
age any age
number 10 or more
time 10 minutes
leaders 2

YOU WILL NEED

- A chair for each child, less one
- Music or a drum

FORMATION

All the chairs placed in a circle facing outwards OR two rows of chairs, back to back OR one row of chairs, alternate ones facing the opposite direction (see picture).

HOW TO PLAY

All players walk around the chairs while the music is playing. When the music stops, the players sit down quickly on a chair. (If you don't have music you can beat a drum rapidly as an alternative.) The player who doesn't find a seat is 'out'. Each time the music starts again, have the child who was 'out' sit on one of the chairs with their arms folded.

WINNER

The winner is the last person in.

LEARNING POINT

It is not nice to be pushed aside and left out.

Poison

space	large
age	8 to 14
number	any number
time	5 to 10 minutes
leaders	1 to 2

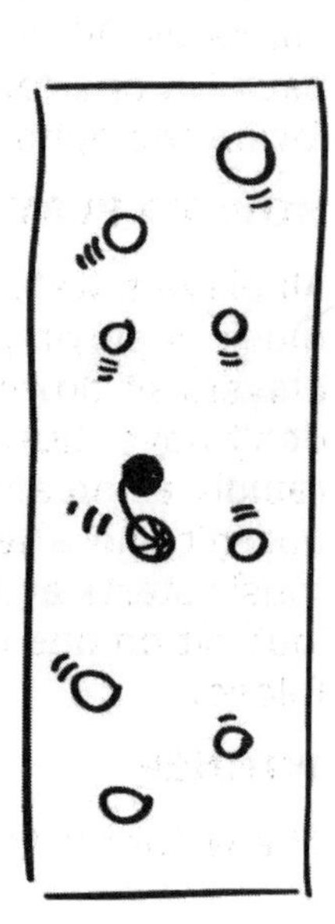

YOU WILL NEED

One ball (large and soft).

FORMATION

Everyone within a marked playing area.

HOW TO PLAY

The leader chases people round the playing area and tries to throw the ball to hit them below the knee. If hit they are dead and have to stay where they are and sit on the floor. The leader will try to see how quickly everyone can be caught.

WINNER

The last person in.

VARIATION

Have two leaders working as a team.

Instead of sitting on the floor when they are caught, they stand with their legs apart. They can then be released by friends who are still 'in' who free them by crawling between their legs.

LEARNING POINTS

- It is a good idea to run away from things that can harm us.
- It is good to try to help others.

Portraits

(similar to 'Wrong Answer')

space	medium
age	8 or above
number	10 to 20
time	10 to 15 minutes
leaders	2

YOU WILL NEED

Nothing.

FORMATION

Everyone sitting round in semicircle — one player to leave the room.

HOW TO PLAY

When the player is outside the room, the players choose the name of a famous person or fictional character, well known to all. Then call in the other player. When he or she comes into the room, he or she has to guess the name of the character by asking questions to the different children, one at a time. The questions can only be answered by 'yes' or 'no' and he or she can ask as many questions as needed. He or she can then have up to three guesses at the identity.

Then another player goes out and another character is chosen.

WINNER

The player(s) who discovers the character.

VARIATION

For younger children, ensure the characters are familiar to that age range.

See 'Wrong Answer'

LEARNING POINT

- How do I know God? How does God know me? What would God say about me?
- If someone had to say what I am like, what would they say?

Statues

space	medium
age	5 to 15
number	10 to 40
time	5 to 10 minutes
leaders	1 to 2

YOU WILL NEED

Music, drum or whistle.

HOW TO PLAY

All run around the area to the music or drum beat. When the music, or drum beat stops, (or when the whistle blows, if there is no music), they have to 'freeze' like statues. The leader(s) then comes around and tries to make them smile, laugh or move, but they must not touch them. Repeat this several times.

WINNER

Is the one who remains a statue the longest.

VARIATION

Not funny (see Team Games).

LEARNING POINTS

It is hard to stick to what you decide is right.

Traffic Lights

space large
age 5 to 14
number any number
time 5 minutes
leaders 2

YOU WILL NEED

Nothing.

FORMATION

Children all along one side of the hall.

HOW TO PLAY

All the children start on one side of the hall with their hand on the wall. The leader explains that he will call out one of three colours.

GREEN will be where they are now.

ORANGE will be in the middle of the hall, and they must quickly move to the middle.

RED will be the opposite side of the hall, in which case they have to run all the way to the other side of the hall.

The last one or two children to get to the correct position will be out.

When half the children are left, add another 'call' which is 'switch'. That simply means that the place for red and green change. So if they are at the GREEN wall and the leader says 'SWITCH GREEN' they run to the opposite wall because the wall they are at has suddenly become RED.

WINNER

The last person in.

VARIATION

You could add other calls such as, Rush Hour, where they find a partner and one has to jump on the other's back! Or, 'Level Crossing' (a level crossing is where a railway track crosses the road!) where the children have to lie on their backs, because a train is coming!

LEARNING POINT

We must think before doing something. The majority may be wrong!

Watch Out

space medium
age 3 to 14
number 10 to 30
time 5 to 10 minutes
leaders 1 to 2

YOU WILL NEED

No equipment

FORMATION

All the children at one end of the hall; a leader at the other end with their back to them.

HOW TO PLAY

All the children have to be in a line at the end of the hall. When the leader turns his back the children start CREEPING QUIETLY towards the leader. The leader will turn round suddenly and anyone who is moving is 'out' and has to sit on the floor exactly where they are. The leader will either point or call the name of the person seen to be moving. If a child runs they are also 'out'.

WINNER

The first child to touch the leader.

VARIATION

Place some obstacles in the way so they have to go round or over them.

LEARNING POINT

Sometimes it is better to go cautiously and thoughtfully in life.

What Am I Doing?

(a miming game)

space	medium
age	11 to 18
number	10 or more
time	10 to 20 minutes
leaders	2

YOU WILL NEED

No equipment.

FORMATION

Those not chosen to leave the room should sit quietly where they can watch.

HOW TO PLAY

3 people are chosen to leave the room. Those left in the room decide on an incident in life that can be acted (bathing the baby, frying an egg, changing a car tyre, catching a bus, catching and plucking a chicken, etc.). The first person is invited back into the room and someone mimes the incident to them. Nothing is to be said verbally. That person has to try and guess what is happening and acts it out to the second person when he comes in and he, in turn, to the 3rd person who then has to say what has been acted.

WINNER

If the 3rd person guesses what the activity was then he has won.

VARIATION

You can have up to 8 children out of the room which can be very funny for those watching.

LEARNING POINT

Some people in life just copy others without bothering to think what is happening. Peer pressure is just copying others so that you won't feel left out.

Who am I?

space	medium
age	11 or above
number	10 to 20
time	10 minutes
leaders	1

YOU WILL NEED

- Names of famous characters written on individual pieces of paper or self-adhesive labels. (one name per label, enough for each child to have one)
- Safety pins, if not using labels

FORMATION

Pin a name on the back of each child without them seeing what it says, (or stick the label on their forehead).

HOW TO PLAY

At the signal, each player goes to another to find out about the name on their piece of paper or label, by asking questions, which can be answered only by 'yes' or 'no'. Then he goes to another and asks another question. When he discovers his identity, he tells the leader.

WINNER

The winner is the first to discover his or her identity.

VARIATION

Need pencils and paper for each child.

The leader to put names on children's backs, when all are standing shoulder to shoulder with eyes closed.

At the signal, they have two minutes to write down as many names on the backs of others as possible, while trying to stop others reading their name.

WINNER

Person with most names is the winner,

AND

Any person whose name has not been seen.

Wrong Answer

(similar to Portraits)

space	medium
age	11 or above
number	10 to 20
time	15 minutes
leaders	1

YOU WILL NEED

Nothing.

HOW TO PLAY

One child leaves the room while the others choose a famous character for them to guess (historical, contemporary, cartoon. etc.). When the child comes back into the room, the leader tells them they can ask one question of each player at a time to find out the name of the famous person. He or she starts by asking the first player, who says nothing. They move on to the next player, who answers the question put to the first player. When they go on to the next player, the answer given is to the previous person's question, and so on. This goes on until they work out the identity of the famous person.

WINNER

The player who guesses the famous person

LEARNING POINTS

Think, to get to the truth.

Yes or No?

(an Icebreaker)

space	small
age	8 or above
number	10 or more
time	5 to 10 minutes
leaders	1

YOU WILL NEED

- 10 matches or beans or small pieces of old newspaper for each person.
- A small prize

HOW TO PLAY

Each player receives 10 used matches, beans or small pieces of paper. Then they go around the room talking to each other, asking questions, without ever using the words 'Yes' or 'No', or nodding or shaking their heads. If they fail, they have to give one match (or bean or paper) to the person they are talking to. After 5 minutes stop the game and have everyone count their matches (or beans or papers). Find out who has the most; then ask who has the least and award them the prize!

When giving the instructions, be careful NOT to tell them the aim of the game.

WINNER

Is the person with the fewest matches or beans or papers. You did not tell them whether they had to win or lose the 10 items. They assumed they had to get as many as possible.

VARIATION

To give children something to talk about give them a list of things to discover about the others they are questioning, such as,

- who has a cat,
- who has four siblings,
- who plays a guitar etc.

LEARNING POINT

- Christianity frequently reverses society's rules. We may have different values to people who are not Christians. The first will be last and the last will be first; the weak are strong the strong weak etc.
- Sometimes you think you are losing (or winning), when you are not!

In a Circle

Circle games are those games where you begin with all players in a circle. Depending on the game they may be facing outwards or inwards, sitting down or standing up. The players need to understand that even when they are 'out', they are not to leave the circle until the game is over.

Break Up

space	medium
age	8 to14
number	30
time	5 minutes
leaders	1

YOU WILL NEED

A mat or ball.

FORMATION

In a circle round the mat or ball.

HOW TO PLAY

Put everyone in a circle linking hands with the children next to them. Advise them to hold onto each other's wrists. (Be careful not to have the youngest children next to the oldest ones, as 14 year–old hands gripping 8 year–old wrists can hurt!)

There is a mat or soft ball in the centre of the circle which if touched results in 'serious sickness'.

When instructed they all move to try and drag someone onto the mat or ball. A person is 'out' if they touch the mat or ball or if they break hands with the person next to them. Continue until there are only three or four left.

WINNER

The last few in the circle.

VARIATION

Require the leaders or older children to hop on one foot so as to make it easier for the younger children.

Change Seats

space	any size
age	8 to 18
number	10 or more
time	10 minutes
leaders	1

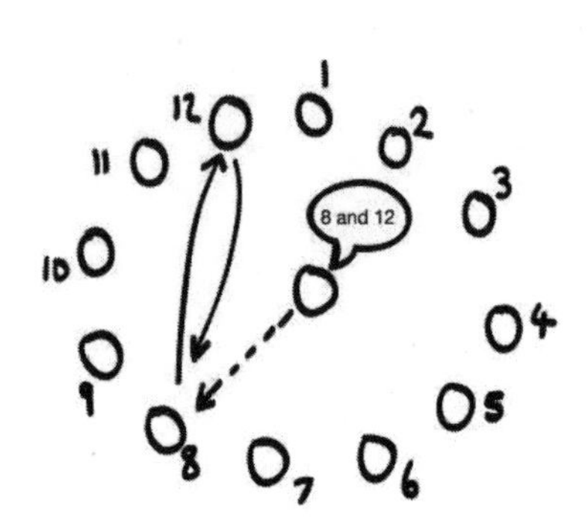

YOU WILL NEED

A chair for everyone; or a circle on the floor, with places marked by cardboard or newspaper so that it is clear where the children sit.

FORMATION

Seated in a circle.

HOW TO PLAY

All but one is seated in a circle. All are numbered 1, 2, 3... etc. including the person in the middle. The one without a seat stands in the centre and explains that, to get a seat he will call out two numbers of people in the circle. These two have to change seats. The person who has called the numbers has to try to sit on an empty seat as the two are changing. Everyone keeps the number they were given at the beginning. (Care is needed as two children may arrive at the seat at the same time at high speed and tip the chair over.)

WINNER

There is no winner. But it's great fun.

VARIATION

You have someone in the centre but you are not numbered. Anyone can wink at another person and they have to change seats. This way you may get four or even six players changing seats at the same time which is fun.

LEARNING POINT

It's not nice to be left out, nor be picked on.

Chocolate Bar

space	any size
age	5 or above
number	12 or more
time	10 to 15 minutes
leaders	1 to 3

YOU WILL NEED

- a chocolate bar wrapped in newspaper and tied with string
- a plate
- a knife and fork
- a jacket
- a dice

FORMATION

Each player sits around a table, or in a circle on the floor. The wrapped chocolate bar is on the plate in the centre, with the knife, fork, scarf and hat.

HOW TO PLAY

The players throw the dice one after another. When the 6 is thrown, the player must quickly put on the jacket and start to unwrap the package using the knife and fork, while the others go on rolling the dice. As soon as another player throws a 6, the first player must stop and give the coat to the new player, and so on. When the players get to the chocolate bar, they may cut small pieces at a time with the knife and fork and eat them. As soon as another person rolls a '6' the first person must stop and let the next person have their turn.

After some time, especially if one or two keep having turns, ask if there is anyone who has not had a turn. If so, you could stop the game and give the remaining chocolate to those who have missed out, or let them take a turn.

WINNER

All can win by getting a piece of chocolate.

VARIATION

This game can be played with a large number of children in teams as a relay race. Make sure you have enough chocolate bars and equipment for each team.

Circle Volleyball

space	medium
age	11 to 18
number	20
time	5 or more minutes
leaders	1

YOU WILL NEED

A large light weight paper ball

FORMATION

A circle with about one metre between each person.

HOW TO PLAY

You have a large but light paper ball (taped). You play volley ball passing the ball between children in the circle. If anyone does a hopeless hit they have to go in the centre of the circle and crouch down. If you miss the ball when you could hit it, you also go into the centre. There may be three or four people in the middle.

If someone in the circle wants to be nasty they can smash the ball (one handed) to hit someone in the centre. If they miss, they too join those in the centre.

You can escape from the centre by trying to catch the ball cleanly and if you do, not only you but everyone in the centre is released.

WINNER

No winner.

LEARNING POINT

All of us may trapped by situations in life and need someone to rescue us.

Fishing Net

space	medium
age	3 to 10
number	12 to 40
time	5 minutes
leaders	1

YOU WILL NEED

Nothing.

FORMATION

Half the children in a circle, the rest standing outside the circle to begin with.

HOW TO PLAY

Half of the children are the fish, the other half form the net. Get those who are the net into a tight circle and whisper a secret number to them, or signal the number using your fingers. When they know the number, they stand in a circle, holding hands high. The leader tells them that when he or she calls the secret number, those who are the net will lower their arms quickly to close the net around the fish inside. The fish run in and out of the net continuously, under the arms of those who are the net. (They cannot stay outside the net just 'to be safe') The leader calls different numbers until the secret number is called. Those fish trapped inside the net become part of the net and a new number is chosen and the game continues. Change over, so that those who were the net to begin with, have a turn at being the fish.

WINNER

The last fish to be caught.

LEARNING POINT

Those who are with you, on your side, can quickly change and turn against you, so choose your friends carefully.

Fizz Buzz

space medium
age 11 or above
number 5 or more
time 10 minutes
leaders 1

YOU WILL NEED

Nothing.

FORMATION

All players sitting in a circle.

HOW TO PLAY

Starting with number one, each player takes turns to say the next number, 1, 2, 3, 4,. Instead of saying 5, the next player must say 'fizz', then the counting continues, 6, 7, 8. All the numbers that are a multiple of 5 (such as 10, 15, 20, 25, 30, 35 etc) must be replaced by 'fizz'. The player who makes a mistake is out.

WINNER

The winner is the last person in.

VARIATION

All numbers with 5 in remain 'fizz', but multiples of 10 (such as 10, 20, 30 etc) are 'buzz'.

Add different variations for older children and make it into a good math's game!

Hat Game

space	medium
age	5 or above
number	15 or more
time	10 minutes
leaders	2

YOU WILL NEED

- 1 or 2 hats, or something to identify the 'sick' person
- a chair for each player

FORMATION

Everyone in a circle, chairs facing inwards. There is one leader, or two if you have more than 20 children playing the game.

HOW TO PLAY

The game begins with everyone sitting on a chair. Nobody must share a seat. There must be no extra seats in the circle.

One or two leaders have a 'sickness' you must not catch, they wear a silly hat (a paper hat perhaps).

When the whistle is blown walk around anywhere inside the circle.

When the whistle is blown again everyone has to sit on a chair, (not two people on one chair).

If they sit next to the 'hat' person they get sick and have to go to hospital and cannot play any more.

The people going to hospital must sit together in the circle, remaining seated until the end of the game.

WINNER

The last two (or four, if playing with two hats) not to catch the sickness are the winners.

LEARNING POINT

There are bad things in the world, even bad people, and we need to be alert and careful to avoid being influenced by them.

Head Catch

space medium
age 8 to 18
number 10 to 30
time 10 minutes
leaders 1 or 2

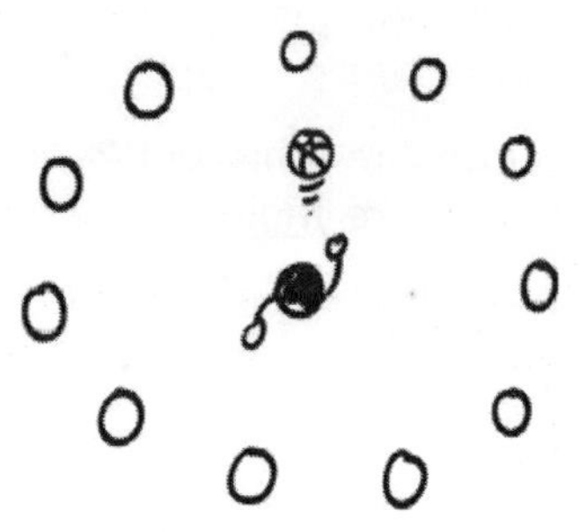

YOU WILL NEED

1 or 2 balls

FORMATION

Circle or half circle. Leader in the centre

HOW TO PLAY

All stand facing the leader in the middle. They start with two or three lives. The leader calls 'catch' or 'head' when throwing the ball to anyone in the circle. That person has to catch or head the ball and return it to the leader. If the ball is caught when it should be headed, or headed when it should be caught, then a 'life' is lost. When all their 'lives' are lost the person either sits down or drops out.

WINNER

The last person to be left. If there are many people you could have the last 5 or 10 left in as joint winners.

VARIATION

Have two leaders each with a ball in the centre of the circle throwing at the same time. This speeds the game up.

After playing the game for 5 minutes tell them that when you call 'catch' they have to 'head' the ball back to the leader and when you say 'head', the ball has to be caught.

LEARNING POINTS

a. To be alert and listen to instructions.

b. Sometimes people will give you wrong instructions. You need to be able to search and identify what truth is. The Bible is a good place to start.

High Throw

space	large
age	8 to 12
number	10 or more
time	5 to 10 minutes
leaders	1 or 2

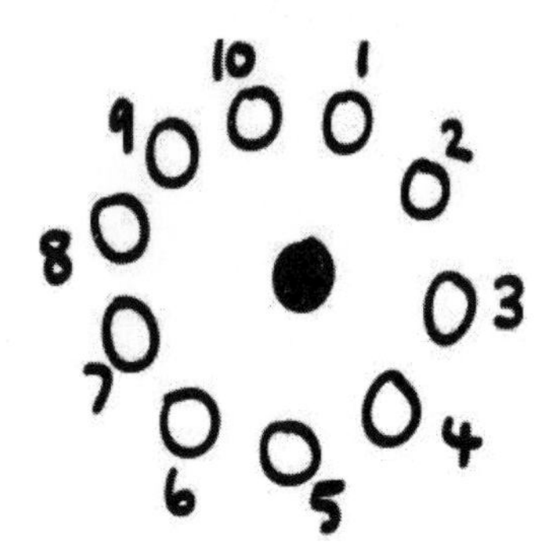

YOU WILL NEED

Large ball.

FORMATION

Circle with one person in the centre.

HOW TO PLAY

Number everyone and stand them in a circle with the leader in the centre. The leader throws the ball above his head and calls out someone's number. That person then has to catch the ball while the others run away.

When the ball is caught the catcher shouts 'Stop!' Everyone must stop running and stand still where they are, while the catcher throws the ball to try and hit one of them. If that person is hit they lose a 'life'. Lives are also lost if someone moves more than one step after the catcher shouts 'stop'.

Each has three lives, then they are out. The children then regroup in a circle for the next round.

WINNER

The last person left in.

VARIATION

When 'out' the 'dead' players stand still but can be thrown the ball from the leader and (if the ball does not touch the ground) can throw the ball to hit someone standing by them.

LEARNING POINTS

Life is not always fair but God gives us all different opportunities.

Lah-di-dah

space	medium
age	8 to 18
number	20
time	5 minutes
leaders	1

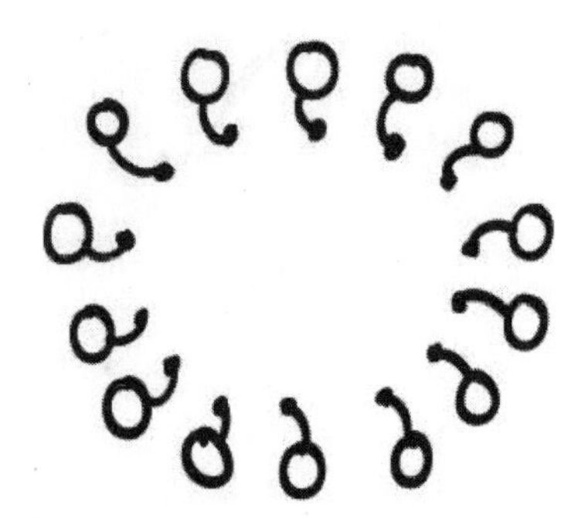

YOU WILL NEED

Enough small, identical unbreakable objects one for each person (spoon or plastic mug, or shoe).

You will need a very observant judge.

FORMATION

Sitting on the ground or round a table.

HOW TO PLAY

Each person playing has a small object in their right hand, which they pass on to the person on their left, at the appropriate moment in the rhythm. You will recite together the following and pass the object on when indicated. 'Lah di dah, lah di dah, lah di dah di dah di dah.'

'Lah *(pick up your object)* di dah' *(put it down on your left)*.

'Lah *(pick up the object on your right which was put down by the person next to you)* di dah' *(put it down on your left)*.

'Lah *(pick up new object from your right)* di dah *(touch it to the table or floor on your left)* di dah *(and touch it to the table or floor on your right)* di dah' *(put it down on your left)*.

On the last line of the refrain you need to touch the object on the table or floor to your left without leaving it there and then to your right, until the third 'dah' is said, when you leave it on your left and pick up the one the person on your right should have left for you.

The refrain continues until someone does not pass their object on, so the person on their left has nothing to pass. Start the refrain very slowly and gradually speed up until someone either goes mad or makes a mistake.

The person 'out' leaves the circle.

WINNER

The last person left in.

Mister Missus

space	small
age	any age
number	6 to 15
time	5 minutes
leaders	1

YOU WILL NEED

A list of masculine words with the corresponding feminine word. For example: boy–girl, man–woman, uncle–aunt, bull–cow, lion–lioness etc.

FORMATION

Everyone in a circle.

HOW TO PLAY

The leader is in the middle of the circle and goes to each player in turn and says a masculine word. The player answers with the corresponding feminine word. If he answers correctly, he gets a point. If he doesn't, the next player can try, and so on.

The leader needs to keep score.

WINNER.

Is the first to get 5 points.

VARIATION

For younger children: choose the names of animals and ask them to tell you what their babies are called (for example cat–kitten etc.).

LEARNING POINTS

- God created us male and female and called us human beings
- God created the animals.

Knee Tap

(an Icebreaker)

space	small
age	8 to 15
number	10 to 30
time	10 minutes
leaders	1

YOU WILL NEED

- A chair for each child
- Baton of rolled up newspaper

FORMATION

The players sit in a circle.

HOW TO PLAY

The leader stands in the middle of the circle. One at a time, the children call each other. For example, 'Anna to Mary'. Mary must then call someone's name, (for example 'Mary to Simon'; then 'Simon to Peter etc.) While Anna is calling Mary, the leader can tap Anna on the knee. If Anna has already called to 'Mary', the leader is too late and must try to hit Mary on the knee before she calls a name, and so on. When he manages to hit someone before they call a name, they take that player's seat and the other player goes in the middle.

WINNER

No winner.

VARIATION

Everyone chooses the name of an animal or a fruit.

LEARNING POINT

- Our names are important.
- God has our name written on the palm of his hand (Isaiah 49:16).

Name Game

(an Icebreaker)

space	medium
age	3 to 12
number	10 to 40
time	5 to 10 minutes
leaders	1 or 2

YOU WILL NEED

A ball.

FORMATION

Get the children to stand in a circle.

Note: if you are playing this game with very young children, have them in a separate group.

HOW TO PLAY

For older children:

Hand a ball to a child on your right and ask him to shout out his name before passing the ball to the next child. (You could also ask them to say what food they like best to eat, or hate to eat.)

When everyone has said their name, the ball is thrown from one to another, shouting: 'Jez to Anna' (for example) and so on around the circle. After they have thrown the ball they sit down on the floor and they should not have the ball thrown to them.

FORMATION

The younger ones should be sitting on the floor for this game and should be limited to a few in number.

HOW TO PLAY

For younger children:

Hand a ball to a child on your right and ask him to shout out his name before passing the ball to the next child.

When everyone has said their name, the ball is rolled from one child to another, and the child rolling the ball should say who they are rolling it to.

Orchestra

space	medium
age	8 or above
number	10 or more
time	10 to 15 minutes
leaders	1

YOU WILL NEED

Nothing.

FORMATION

All players sitting in a circle, except child A who goes out of the room.

HOW TO PLAY

One child goes out of the room. Another child in the circle is chosen to be the orchestra conductor, whom all the others imitate. The conductor mimes playing an instrument such as the violin. All the other children copy by playing the violin. The conductor then switches to miming another instrument such as trumpet or drum or flute, etc. All the others copy whatever the conductor chooses to play.

The child who was sent out returns to the room and stands in the middle of the circle. The leader explains that he must guess who is making the orchestra change their actions The orchestra keeps playing until the child in the centre has guessed correctly.

Once the conductor has been guessed correctly, this child rejoins the circle, then another child leaves the room while a new conductor is chosen, and the game repeated.

VARIATION

The conductor could make any body movement, arm, leg or head which has to be copied by the rest, like tapping the end of his nose.

WINNER

No–one.

Pass it On

space large
age 8 to 18
number 20 or more
time 5 minutes
leaders 2

YOU WILL NEED

- baton (rolled up newspaper) or a ball
- a chair for each child

FORMATION

For this game you must put the chairs in a big circle, but turn them around so that they are all facing outwards.

HOW TO PLAY

When the whistle is blown, an object (such as a baton or ball) is passed from person to person around the outside of the circle.

When the whistle is blown again, the one holding the object being passed is 'out'.

The player who is 'out' must not leave the circle but turns his seat to face the centre instead, He must not touch the baton or ball. The other players must pass the item round him on the outside. The players who are out just sit and watch.

As more and more are out of the game, the remaining players will need to get out of their chairs and run round the outside of the circle to reach the next player. It is not permitted to throw the object to the next player, it must be passed.

The leader with the whistle should keep their back to the players when blowing the whistle. Another leader should keep watch on the game.

WINNER

The last one or two still in.

VARIATION

If many people are playing have two batons or balls circulating at the same time.

Peter and Mary

space	medium
age	8 to 14
number	12 to 20
time	10 minutes
leaders	1

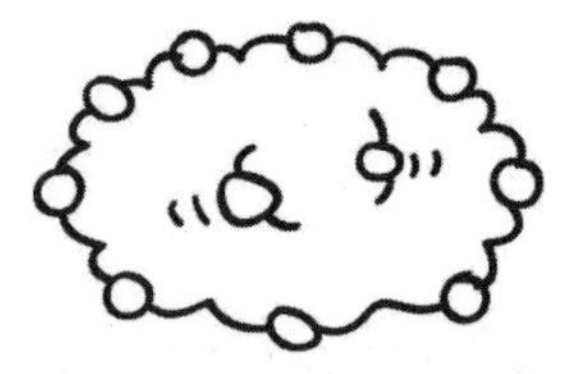

YOU WILL NEED

2 blindfolds.

FORMATION

Everyone standing in a big circle, holding hands.

HOW TO PLAY

The goal of the game is for 'Peter' to catch 'Mary' within one minute. Everybody must be very quiet. 'Peter' and 'Mary' are blindfolded and stand inside the circle formed by everyone else. Peter calls Mary. She replies, 'I'm Mary' and then tries to escape from him. He calls her until he touches her. Then another pair can have a turn.

WINNER

'Peter', if he catches her within one minute, or 'Mary' if he doesn't.

LEARNING POINT

Don't run away from Jesus when He calls you. You are safe with him. He loves you!

Pole Catch

space	medium
age	8 to 18
number	10 to 20
time	10 minutes
leaders	1

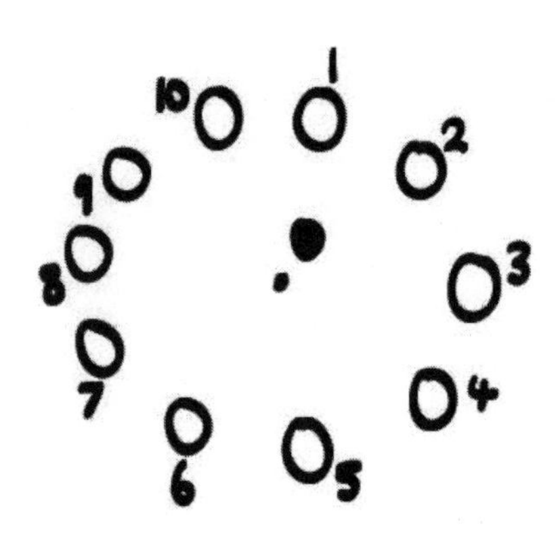

YOU WILL NEED

Stick or brush handle one metre long.

FORMATION

Seated in a circle with 'caller' standing in the centre with a pole.

HOW TO PLAY

Everyone in the circle is numbered. The 'caller' calls out a number and at the same time, lets go of the top of the stick so it starts to fall. The person whose number was called has to catch the pole before it hits the ground. If they catch it the caller stays in the centre and calls another number. If you don't catch it you become the caller in the centre. The caller must not push the pole over!

WINNER

Those who caught the stick before it hit the ground.

VARIATION

Instead of saying 8 you can say 4 plus 4 if the children can manage that. Also, you can call a number and look at the wrong person which confuses the one who should come forward.

LEARNING POINTS

Sometimes you may have to make quick decisions in life. It is vital that they are the right ones.

Ring on a String

space	medium
age	8 to 14
number	10 to 30
time	10 minutes
leaders	1

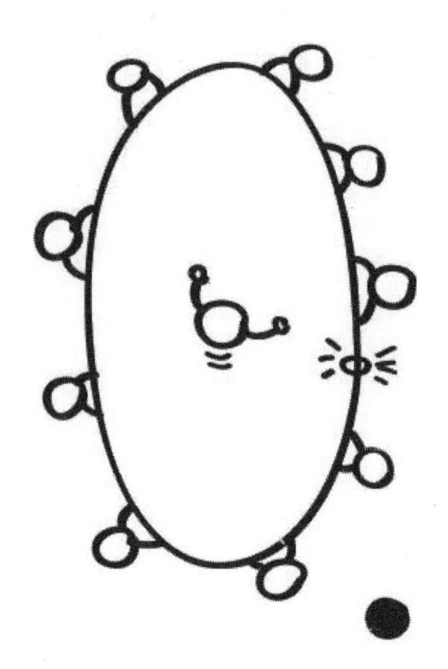

YOU WILL NEED

A small ring or a key threaded onto a circle of string.

FORMATION

Stand in a circle with hands on the string. The 'seeker' stands in the centre.

HOW TO PLAY

Everyone stands in a circle holding the string. The one in the centre (the 'seeker') closes their eyes and is turned around a couple of times by the leader while the ring is moved round the string. When the seeker is told to open his or her eyes, the game starts.

The ring has to be passed continually around the string by the players in the circle. Even those who do not have the ring should pretend to pass the ring round.

The seeker in the centre has to guess who has the ring by tapping someone's hands (the person has to lift their hands off the string to show whether they have it). If the person is 'caught' with the ring, they then take the place of the seeker in the centre, and the game repeated.

WINNER

The seekers who find the ring.

VARIATION

Limit the seeker to ten attempts at finding the ring and then choose someone else to be in the centre.

Smash

space	medium
age	5 to 14
number	30
time	5 minutes
leaders	1

YOU WILL NEED

Rolled up newspaper, maximum two pages thick.

FORMATION

In a close circle, facing inwards.

HOW TO PLAY

Get all the players in a close circle with their hands behind their backs, open and ready to receive a rolled up paper baton, (2 sheets and taped). Players should shut their eyes.

The leader starts the game by walking slowly round the circle and without breaking pace slips the paper stick into the hand of any person. The one receiving the stick can then start hitting the person on their right with the paper baton. The one being hit must run round the circle as fast as they can to avoid the person chasing them, and return to the safety of their place in the circle.

On return to the circle the victim takes the newspaper and walks quietly round the circle as happened before.

WINNER

No winners.

LEARNING POINT

Be ready for the unexpected!

Snake Bite

space	medium
age	8 to 14
number	5 to 30
time	5 to 10 minutes
leaders	1

YOU WILL NEED

- Rope or thick cord.
- Soft weight like an old shoe tied to the end of the rope.

FORMATION

Standing in a circle.

HOW TO PLAY

The leader stands in the centre of the circle holding the rope (snake) and swings it round in a big circle at ankle height. Everyone needs to jump over it as it goes round and round. If it snags round someone's leg they are out, and they have to leave the circle.

WINNER

Is the last one to be left in the circle. If you have a large number of players, you may decide to play until the last five are left in, and these will be the winners.

LEARNING POINT

As you need to jump before the rope gets to you so you need to be ready in advance to meet problems in life.

Wink Death

space	small
age	8 to 14
number	10 to 30
time	10 minutes
leaders	1

YOU WILL NEED

A small piece of paper for each participant, one with an 'X' marked on it.

FORMATION

Circle, all players sitting so they can see each other.

HOW TO PLAY

Everyone is secretly given a piece of folded paper which are all blank except one which has a cross on it. The child who receives the paper with the cross on it is the murderer, who 'kills' people by winking at them without the others noticing. If you have been winked at you have been murdered and can die a terrible death (be dramatic, groan and, maybe, collapse on the floor).

The object is that everyone is trying to find out who the murderer is before they are killed themselves. If a player thinks they see someone winking at someone else they are to say loudly, 'YOU ARE THE MURDERER'. If the accusation is correct the game is over and the pieces of paper are re-distributed. If wrong the accuser dies, and the game continues.

WINNER

Is the person who kills most people before they are discovered.

VARIATION

Add a piece of paper which has a star (*) on it. The person with the star is the detective and alone has to identify the murderer.

Zip Zap Boing Pow

space medium
age 11 to 18
number 20
time 5 minutes
leaders 1

YOU WILL NEED

Nothing.

FORMATION

Sitting in a circle

HOW TO PLAY

You play this by passing 'nothing' from person to person in the following way. Put your hands together with your two fore-fingers pointing out like a gun.

Zip: you start off in one direction both pointing your two fingers, and looking at the person you are passing the zip to, who is the person next to you. The person receiving the zip passes it on in the same way.

Zap: If someone has passed a zip to you, you can pass it back to them by saying 'zap' and it then the zip continues in the other direction.

Boing: This skips one person to the person beyond the one sitting next to you.

Pow: To use this you lift your clenched hand up above your head and say 'pow' while pointing with your other hand and making eye contact with someone across the circle. They then pass the zip on in any direction they like.

You must not pow or boing someone who has just pow'ed or boing'ed you or to anyone who is out.

You are out if you hesitate or look in the wrong direction or pass to someone who is already out.

Start with just the zip and zap and introduce the boing and pow later.

WINNER

Is the last two people left in.

LEARNING POINT

When under pressure you still need to make the right decisions.

In Groups

Most of the group games are played with children in teams each seated in semi–circle in a different corner of the playing area.

Cross Arms

space	medium
age	8 or above
number	6 to 30
time	5
leaders	1

YOU WILL NEED

Nothing.

FORMATION

Groups of 6, of similar height.

HOW TO PLAY

As many groups of 6 as possible. Stand facing each other in their circle. All raise their left hand and take the left hand of someone else across from them. Now raise their right hand and take the right hand of a different person in the circle. They must not hold the hands of the same person.

When you give the word, they must try and untangle themselves, (without letting go of their hands at any time) and open out into a larger circle. Some may end up with their backs to the rest of them and that is fine.

They must not let go of the others' hands at any time during the activity, though they may adjust their grip.

WINNER

The winner is the first team to unravel their circle.

LEARNING POINTS

Many people facing a problem don't talk about it. In this game it is important to work together.

Draw It

space	large
age	8 to 18
number	12 to 40
time	10 to 15 minutes
leaders	2

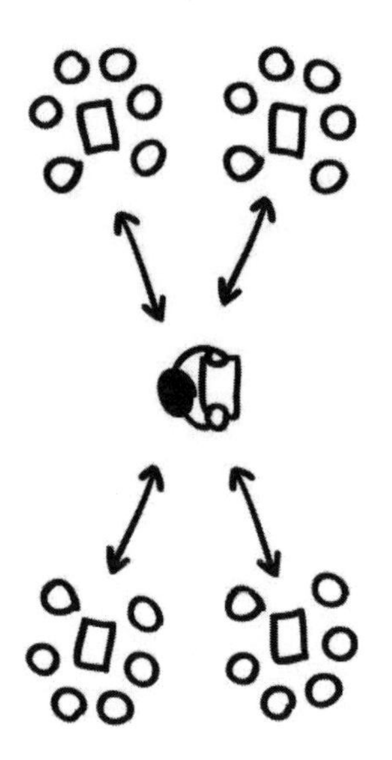

YOU WILL NEED

Blank paper and pen or pencil for each team OR if outside, stick and sand to draw in.

FORMATION

Four teams in different corners of the playing area. Four to eight people per team is ideal.

HOW TO PLAY

A leader stands in the centre of the room with a list of objects to be drawn. The objects must be simple for young children, for example: house, man, lady, tree, sun, moon, snake, bird. For older children they can be more challenging!

The game starts by each group sending one person out to the leader who whispers to all four at the same time what they are to draw. (This is the only time they are told the object at the same time). The children run back to their groups and start drawing the object. They may NOT speak nor write numbers or letters or words, nor may they mime.

When someone guesses correctly what is being drawn, the next person in the team runs out and tells the leader what was drawn. The leader checks the list and gives out the next object to be drawn and so on until a team reaches the end.

WINNER

The first team to draw and correctly guess all items on the leader's list wins.

VARIATION

If the children have problems drawing they can be allowed to speak but not allowed to say the name of the thing being drawn.

The leader with the list could move to different places in or outside the playing area so they have to be found by the children.

LEARNING POINT

Sometimes it is important to watch and listen.

Find a Word

space small
age 11 or above
number 12 or more
time 10 minutes
leaders 1

R rhubarb

E excellent

G gyrate

A …

L

YOU WILL NEED

- blackboard and chalk, or similar
- paper and pencil for each team

FORMATION

Teams in each corner of the playing area.

HOW TO PLAY

The leader writes a word vertically on the blackboard, downwards.

Each team must think of words that start with the letters in each row, the first one starting with the first letter given, the second word starting with the second letter given and so on.

WINNER

Is the quickest team to complete all the words.

OR

If more than one team has the same word: no score for this word.

If no other team has the same word: 5 points for each unique word.

See which team has the highest score.

VARIATION

The challenge can be to think of a fruit for each letter of the alphabet for round 1; round 2 can be towns; round 3 boy's names, and so on.

LEARNING POINT

God has created such a variety of wonderful things and people, some common, some unusual, some rare but all special to God.

Find it, Bring it

space	large
age	8 to 18
number	12 to 40
time	10 to 15 minutes
leaders	1 or more

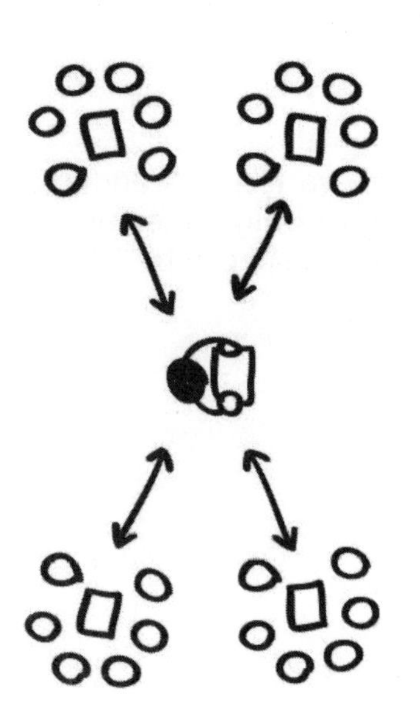

YOU WILL NEED

Nothing.

FORMATION

Four groups round the hall in semi circles.

HOW TO PLAY

The leader calls out an item for the groups to bring to him or her. (Some examples: someone wearing red, a shoe, a sock, a blade of grass, the biggest person carried out by the rest of the team, two shoes tied together, piece of paper, leaf of a tree, a 10 year old boy, a coin, someone's hair-band, a leader etc.)

The first person to reach the leader with the item scores a point for their team. Then the next item is called for, and so on. The items don't count if worn by the courier.

WINNER

Is the team with the highest score.

LEARNING POINTS

Sometimes in life you have to work quickly and as a team.

Grab It

(like Shoes)

space	large
age	8 to 18
number	12 to 40
time	10 to 15 minutes
leaders	2 or more

YOU WILL NEED

- 7 small objects, match box size (stones, sticks, shells or small balls of taped paper)
- 4 chairs or similar
- table or box or similar

FORMATION

Four groups, each one lined up behind a chair. The chairs are all the same distance from a table or box in the centre, on which are 7 items. The chairs must be evenly spaced from each other (see diagram above).

HOW TO PLAY

The children in the groups are numbered from front to back. The youngest stand in the front.

When a number is called that person, from each group, runs to the centre and picks up one item and takes it back and places it on their chair. The player then returns for another and another. When there are three items on the chair that group has won. If there are not enough in the centre to make up the number, items can be stolen one at a time from the chairs of the other groups. No one can stop this theft! All the items must be taken from the middle first.

The first team to have three items on their chair scores a point for their team.

Strict control should be attempted as it is almost impossible not to cheat!

WINNER

The group with the highest score.

VARIATION

The game can be made faster and longer if the leader removes an item from the centre, leaving just six. For younger children the number of items can be increased to make it easier for them.

LEARNING POINTS

We must be in control of ourselves, The temptation to do wrong is always there.

Identify Me!

(like charades)

space	medium
age	11 to 18
number	12 to 36
time	20 minutes
leaders	1

YOU WILL NEED

- pencils for everyone
- 3 small pieces of paper for everyone
- timer
- hat or container to collect the papers

FORMATION

Divide into 2 to 4 groups, sitting together.

HOW TO PLAY

Everyone think of three characters (which everyone will know) alive, dead or fictional (can be cartoon characters) and write them on individual slips of paper. Fold the papers twice so no–one else can see what is written and put them in a hat or container.

Round 1: One group starts and has 30 second to play. A player takes a name from the hat and describes it to their group without saying the word on the paper. The group listen and if they guess correctly they keep that name and the player takes another name to describe continuing until their time runs out. The group must guess as many of the names as possible.

The other groups then get a chance in the same way keeping the papers they guess within a 30 second time limit. When the names are all used the groups count how many they have before folding them and replacing them in the container. The leader notes the score for each team.

Round 2: Same as round 1, except only one word can be used to describe the name on the paper.

Round 3: No words at all can be said. The character must be mimed. This is easier than it seems as everyone has heard all the names twice already.

WINNER

Is the team with the highest score.

LEARNING POINT

Will we be remembered for good or bad things we have done?

Mad Football

space large
age 8 to 18
number 16
time 10 minutes
leaders 5

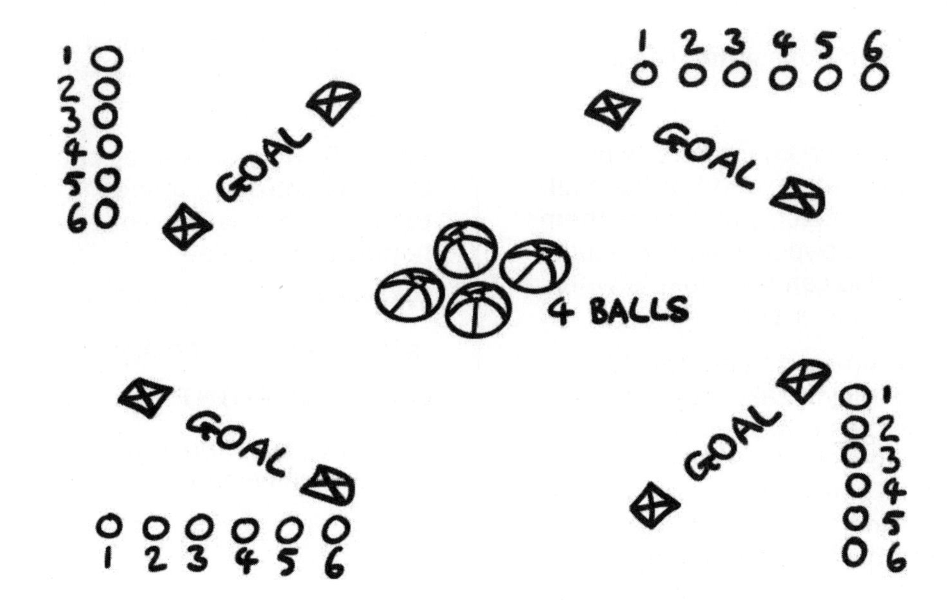

YOU WILL NEED

- 4 soft balls
- 8 markers for goals
- a very strict referee

FORMATION

This is football with 4 teams playing at the same time. All teams stay behind their goal, as per the diagram, and are numbered off from one upwards.

HOW TO PLAY

Four teams are against the wall and three numbers are called. There will be four goals equally spaced about three metres wide (coats or chairs). In the centre there are four or more balls. When the whistle is blown the players who have had their numbers called can leave their goal mouth and try to score a goal in one of the other goals. Any pushing, barging or handling of the ball and the offender leaves the field for 30 seconds. A team may decide to leave one of their players in their goal mouth as a goal-keeper.

You will need a leader behind each goal to count how many balls come through the goal — 5 points for each goal.

The referee has to be very strict and the game must stop when he blows the whistle. When a goal is scored the leader behind that goal puts that ball back into the centre.

After three minutes the players are changed and another three numbers are called.

Be careful to try to make sure that girls do not compete against boys so the numbering is very important.

WINNER

Is the team with the lowest score, since they will have let in the fewest goals.

Make it Come Alive

(a Bible game)

space	large
age	11 to 18
number	40
time	20 minutes
leaders	3

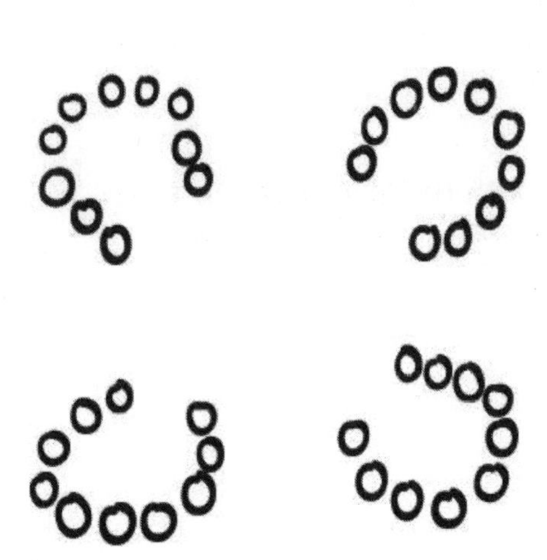

YOU WILL NEED

- 3 newspapers for each group
- sticking tape

FORMATION

In 2 or 4 groups (depending on numbers). 10 children in a group.

HOW TO PLAY

Each group has 20 minutes to carry out the following task:

- One person read the Bible passage to the others in the team.
- Make something which appears in the verses you have been given. (award points out of 10 maximum)
- Dramatize the event as best you can in a three minute theatrical presentation. (points out of 20 maximum)
- One person takes 30 seconds to explain, in very simple and clear language, what the importance of the passage is. This is for the benefit of the members of the other three groups who are watching and listening, and should assume that they know nothing of the story or context. (maximum 30 points)
- Use lots of active expression. (up to 10)
- Keep within time limit. (up to 10 points)

Here are some possible verses to use:

1. Genesis 6 v 12 to 18 *(Flood: Noah's ark)*
2. Genesis 11 v 4 to 11 *(Tower of Babel)*
3. Matt 14 v 25 to 32 *(Walking on water: boat)*
4. Luke 23 v 33 to 43 *(Crucifixion: cross)*

Ensure a leader is available to help answer any questions the group may raise.

WINNER

Is the team with the highest score.

LEARNING POINT

The Bible is full of stories about life, which are relevant and helpful to us today.

Memory

space	medium
age	8 to 18
number	10 to 40
time	15 minutes
leaders	4 to 5 ideal

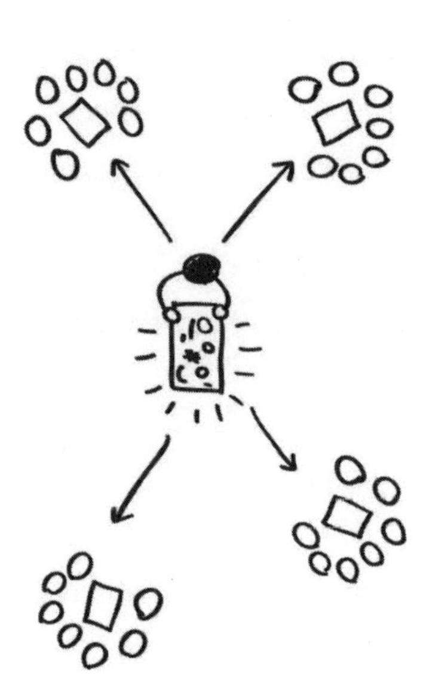

YOU WILL NEED

- Tray or similar, with 10 to 20 small items (pen, watch, match, leaf, etc.)
- Cloth or paper to cover the tray
- Paper and pencil for each group

FORMATION

In small groups around the playing area.

HOW TO PLAY

The items are placed on a tray and are taken to each group. The group can look at them for 10 seconds (they must not touch them). After everyone has seen the items and the tray is removed, the group is given two minutes to make one list of all the items they can remember. They must not shout the items out or the other groups may hear.

Take the tray to the next group and repeat the process. Remember to ensure all teams have an equal amount of time to write their answers.

WINNER

Call out the items on the tray while groups check their list. The one with the most things listed wins.

VARIATION

Show the items to all the children at the same time and after 10 seconds cover them up and ask each group in turn to call an item out. Keep a score.

When you have those who cannot write, play it this way...

Show them the tray of items, as above, then remove the tray from sight and take away a couple of items. Bring the tray back and the first team to identify a missing item scores a point. Replace those items and remove others, etc.

LEARNING POINTS

Everything in life is important even the little things.

Mime Competition

(a Bible game)

space	large
age	8 or above
number	12 to 40
time	10 minutes
leaders	2

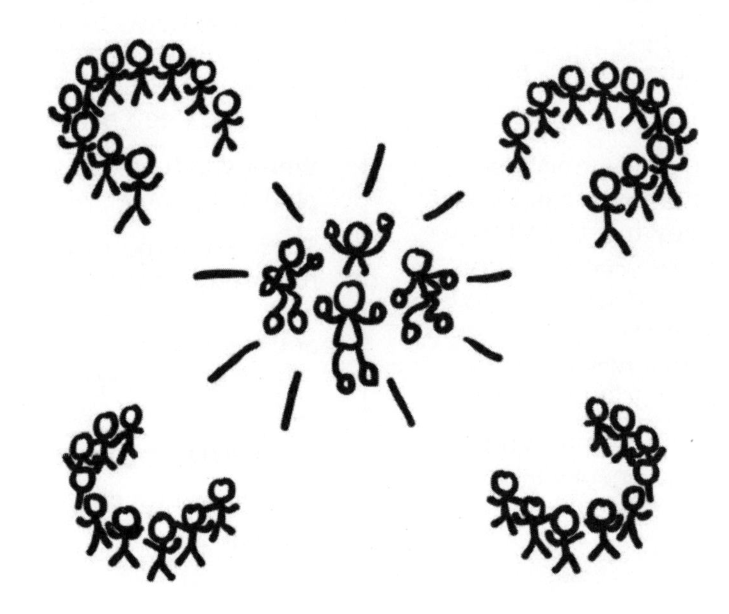

YOU WILL NEED

Paper and pencil for each group.

FORMATION

If possible have the groups form four semi-circles with their chairs, one in each corner of the playing area. This should be done so that participants can talk to other members of their group, but also be able to see the other groups. There needs to be space in the centre for drama activity.

HOW TO PLAY

Tell everyone that they have three minutes to make a list of as many Bible stories as they can. Then:

- Taking it in turns, each group mimes a Bible story.
- The other groups shout out what they think is being acted. The first group to guess it gets a point.
- The next group then does a different Bible story, and so on.
- They are not allowed to repeat a story that has already been done.
- This continues until a group repeats one already done, or cannot perform, when they are 'out'.

A group has to start acting within 10 seconds of the group which has just finished.

WINNER

One winner is the team with the highest score. Another is the final team still in.

VARIATION

The challenge could be for them to mime traditional folk stories or nursery rhymes.

LEARNING POINT

It is good to enjoy your Bible stories.

Shoes

(like Grab It)

space	large
age	8 or above
number	12 to 20
time	10 minutes
leaders	2 or more

YOU WILL NEED

- a blindfold for each team
- a chair or stool for each team

FORMATION

Each group lined up behind a chair or similar, which is the same distance from a marked area in the centre. The chairs must be evenly spaced from each other.

The first person in each team is blindfolded.

HOW TO PLAY

This game can only be played if culturally acceptable.

The children remove their shoes and pile them up in the centre of the room.

At a signal, the first person in each team crawls to the heap in the centre of the room and takes ONE shoe at a time back to his seat. He can be guided by the rest of his team. He can also steal shoes from his neighbours, but only ONE at a time. The first team to have a matching pair of shoes shouts 'stop'. 5 points are awarded for the pair of shoes and 1 point to each team for each shoe they have before returning them all to the centre. The next player in each group then takes a turn with the blindfold etc.

WINNER

Is the team with the highest score.

Sword Fight

space	medium
age	7 to 15
number	4 at a time
time	8 minutes
leaders	1

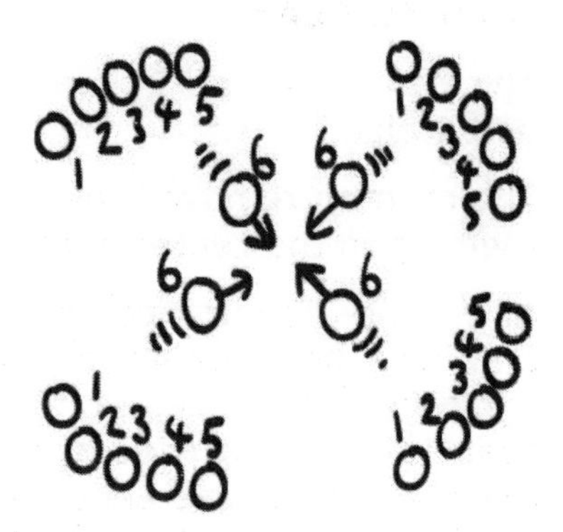

YOU WILL NEED

- 4 pieces of flat cardboard or tin trays
- 4 swords (rolled up and taped newspaper — two pages thick)

FORMATION

The children should be in their four teams in corners of the hall. One person comes in to fight from each team with a sword (rolled up double sheet of taped newspaper) and a shield (a flat piece of cardboard about the size of a large sheet of paper, or a tin tray) which has to be balanced on an open hand (not held in the hand).

HOW TO PLAY

Everyone in the teams is numbered starting at the youngest (or smallest).

When a number is called that person comes out with sword and shield to fight. When someone's shield is knocked to the floor that person is out of the game. The winner is the survivor of the contest and they win 10 points for their team.

Try to give everyone a turn.

WINNER

Is the team with the highest score.

VARIATION

Try it with the four children blindfolded.

LEARNING POINT

The Bible tells us to put on armour from God to survive in this world. We do not need to use guns and knives or other weapons.

Relay Races

Relays are made up of two or more teams of the same number of players, playing in parallel. (For example four teams of ten players each.) Each player on the team takes their turn in the activity until all have played.

Ball Roll

space	large
age	5 to 14
number	40
time	5 minutes
leaders	3

YOU WILL NEED

- 4 balls
- 4 chairs
- leaders to keep score

FORMATION

Children to be in teams with a chair 5 metres in front of each team.

HOW TO PLAY

When the whistle is blown the first person in each team tries to either hit the chair or roll the ball through the legs of the chair in front. When they have done that the person throwing retrieves the ball and gives it to the next in line before running to the back of the team. The next person then tries and so on until all have had a go.

Five points are given for hitting the chair, ten points for getting the ball through the chairs legs. There is an extra ten points for the first team to finish.

WINNER

Is the team with the highest score.

VARIATION

Place the chairs closer and put a container on the seat. The objective would be to make the ball land in the container.

LEARNING POINT

Take care in life that you are aiming in the right direction.

Bible Footsteps

space large
age 5 to 10
number 36
time 5 minutes
leaders 2

YOU WILL NEED

- ten numbered footprints for each team, with the verse (split into ten parts) written on the reverse of one set only
- two lines marking out a river

FORMATION

In four teams with a pile of ten prepared footprints on the ground in front of each team.

HOW TO PLAY

The first challenge is for each team to put the footprints across the river (marked by the two lines on the floor), in the right order (starting at 1 and ending at 10). Then the whole team must cross the river, stepping only on the footprints, the last player picking up the footprints on the way. They will be given points if they do not get their feet wet (by stepping on the floor). Give points for the first team to finish and sit quietly.

Now get all the teams to sit down except for the winning team who stand in front of the others. Give them the set of cards with the verse on, and starting with number 1 they turn the cards round one by one until the whole verse is visible.

Everyone repeat the verse:

> The fruit of the Spirit is
> love, joy, peace,
> patience, kindness, goodness,
> faithfulness, gentleness and
> self control.
> Galatians 5 v 22–23

Now help them to memorize the verses, removing one footprint each time.

VARIATION

Do it with 1 Corinthians 13 v 4 to 7 or any other you wish to learn.

LEARNING POINT

The verse on the footprints.

Bible Text Relay

space	large
age	8 to 14
number	12 or more
time	10 minutes
leaders	2 minimum

YOU WILL NEED

The Bible verse written on large sheets of paper, one for each team. Cut these sheets of paper into 10 or 12 irregular pieces as per diagram.

(Use different colour pens or paper for each team. It helps to put the verses into separate envelopes so that they don't get muddled.)

FORMATION

Equal teams at one end of area, verses at the other.

HOW TO PLAY

Have a chair opposite each team with a cut-up verse on it. At the other end of the room have the teams in line. In turn, they run up to pick up one piece of text and take it to the back of their team. When all the pieces are collected, they must put them together to work out the verse.

WINNER

First team to complete the verse.

Extra points for:

- first person or team to memorize the verse, and
- to explain what the verse is trying to tell us today.

LEARNING POINT

Make sure you understand what a Bible verse means for you today.

Bible Quiz

space	medium
age	5 to 14
number	12 or more
time	5 to 10 minutes
leaders	2

YOU WILL NEED

- a list of questions
- someone to keep score

FORMATION

2 to 4 teams, sitting in rows, youngest at the front, oldest at the back.

HOW TO PLAY

The first person in each team is asked the first question. First to raise their hand answers. If they get it right, they score a point for their team. The next question goes to the second in each team, and so on.

Make sure that the stories you choose questions from have been covered recently in your teaching.

WINNER

Is the team with the highest score.

VARIATION

You can use other themes, such as general knowledge, nature, hygiene etc.

Ask the first question to one team, if they answer correctly they score a point, otherwise, another team can answer and score. The next question goes to the next team and so on.

Car Race

space	large
age	6 to 18
number	40
time	5 minutes
leaders	2

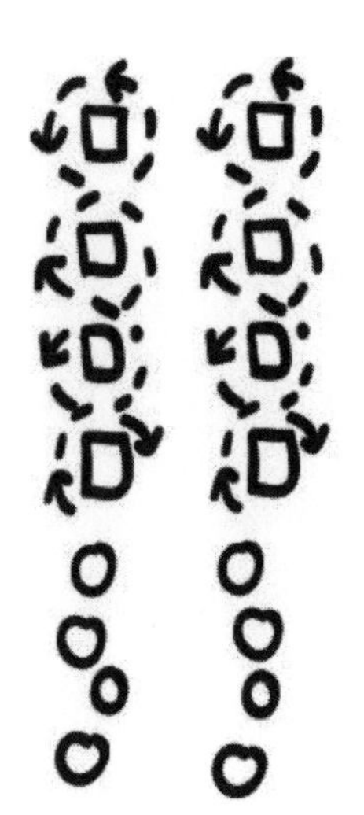

YOU WILL NEED

- Sticks, lids or card for cars for each team
- 4 chairs or obstacles for each team
- 4 or 8 blindfolds

Optional: 4 small potatoes, spoons, or balloons.

FORMATION

Children in teams, lined up at one end of hall.

HOW TO PLAY

Put four chairs out, one in front of each team spaced about a metre between each other. Children take it in turn to drive their car, (a jam jar lid or a piece of cardboard, — anything) steering it with a thin bamboo stick, or newspaper roll, round the chairs and back to their team. The child also has to be blindfolded and guided by someone who stays back behind the team line. If you have a spare blindfold for each team have the next person blindfolded before the first driver returns to keep things moving.

WINNER

Is the first team back and sitting quietly.

VARIATION

Play it without being blindfolded, just with the car and stick but they also have to have a potato balanced on a spoon in the other hand. If the potato falls off they have to put it on and carry on from where they left off. The spoon, potato, car and stick are handed to the next person in the team to carry on until everyone has had a go.

In addition to the above make them walk with a balloon between their legs.

LEARNING POINT

There will be a lot of people telling you what you should do in life. You must listen to the right voices.

Chain Run

space large
age 8 to 18
number 10 to 40
time 5 minutes
leaders 1

YOU WILL NEED

4 markers (could be a chair or a leader)

FORMATION

Four equal teams with the smallest at the front, tallest at the back (maximum ten in a team). Each team spaced about three metres from the other teams.

HOW TO PLAY

At the word 'go' the first player runs round a marker and back to the end of the team. As he passes, he touches the next one (who then starts running) while he returns to the end of the team. The game stops when the first runner is back at the front of the team.

WINNER

The first team to be back where they started from.

VARIATION

Try it running backwards; hopping or skipping. Try carrying an item with you and passing it on before the next one runs.

LEARNING POINTS

- Life can involve a lot of running about and getting nowhere. How can you have somewhere, something to aim at?
- Jesus gives meaning and purpose to what we do and where we go.

Chariots

space	large
age	7 to 18
number	60
time	5 minutes
leaders	5

YOU WILL NEED

- 4 balls
- 4 boxes or buckets or bins of equal size

FORMATION

Four teams of up to 15 in each team. Four leaders at the end of the hall to retrieve the balls.

HOW TO PLAY

Each team needs to divide their members into threes. One in each trio should be smaller than the others.

Two of the trio hold hands making a seat. The third person (smallest) sits on the 'seat' with a ball in his hands. At the whistle the four chariots go to the end of the hall and the rider drops his ball into a box or bin. If it stays in it is 5 points. A leader hands the ball back to the rider and they drive back to their team handing the ball to the next chariot.

If children do not split neatly into three's then one or two children may go twice.

WINNER

Is the team with the highest score after all of the chariots have had their turn.

VARIATION

Leave the balls and just have the chariots go round a chair or leader at the end of the hall

LEARNING POINT

We need each other to succeed in life.

Cross the River

space	large
age	5 or above
number	10 to 24
time	10 to 15 minutes
leaders	1 or 2

YOU WILL NEED

- for each team, 3 mats or pieces of cardboard or sheets of newspaper
- 2 lines for the river (marked with chalk or tape or string)

FORMATION

Divide into equal teams of 4 or 5 players each. The teams stand in rows behind a line.

HOW TO PLAY

Each player in the team, in turn, has to cross the river by stepping only on the pieces of cardboard provided. Having crossed the river one way, he runs back and gives the three pieces of card to the next player who does the same. If he falls in the river, he must start again.

WINNER

Is the first team to cross the river.

VARIATION

If you have chairs, the whole team has to cross together on chairs. A chair for each member of the team and they all cross at the same time.

For older children, the challenge can be to cross together and transfer objects (like a bowl of water) as well!

LEARNING POINT

The Lord tells us to follow in His footsteps.

Donkey's Tail

space	medium
age	3 to 10
number	16 to 20
time	10 minutes
leaders	3 to 4

YOU WILL NEED

For each team:

- a large drawing of the donkey's rear (without its tail) on the front wall
- a blindfold
- donkey's tail with a drawing pin or a crayon to mark the spot

FORMATION

Each team in line facing the picture of the donkey.

HOW TO PLAY

Blindfold the first child in each team and give them the tail and pin or crayon. They must walk straight ahead and pin the tail on the donkey's rear, or mark where the tail should be with the crayon. They can be guided by the leader to the donkey or by the rest of their team. If using the tail, the leader must mark the spot before the tail is taken back to the team for the next player, who is then blindfolded, etc.

WINNER

Is the team who got the tail in the right place (or nearest).

LEARNING POINT

We often need other people's help in order to do a better job.

Fun Relay

(a Bible verse game)

space	large
age	8 or above
number	12 or more
time	5 minutes
leaders	2

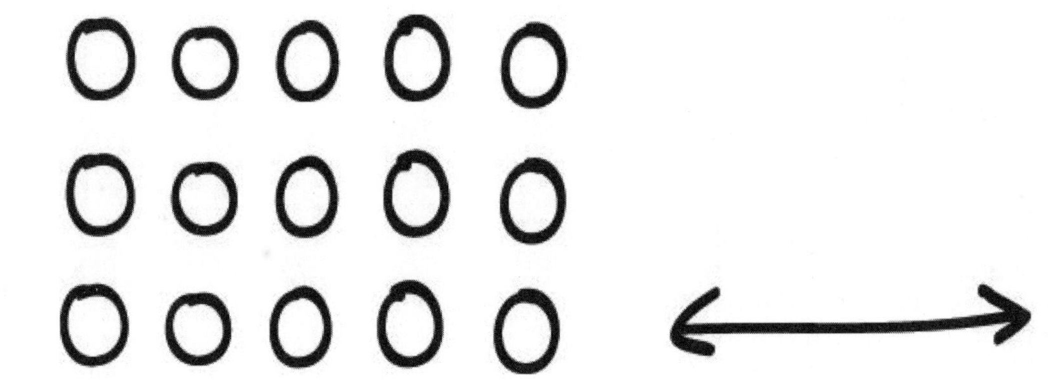

YOU WILL NEED

Adult coat for each team (optional)

FORMATION

Equal teams in straight lines. Each team faces a chair with an adult coat on it.

HOW TO PLAY

First get the children in their teams to learn a memory verse together.

Line the children up in relay teams. When the whistle blows the first child in each team runs forward and puts on the oversized coat. They then stand on the chair and shout the verse out to the others in their team. When they have said it correctly, they take off the coat and run back to their team. Then the next child in the team has a turn.

If the player with the coat has trouble recalling the memory verse, the team can help their player by shouting out the words as a reminder.

WINNER

The first team to finish.

Mass Exhaustion

space large
age 8 to 18
number 10 to 40
time 5 minutes
leaders 2

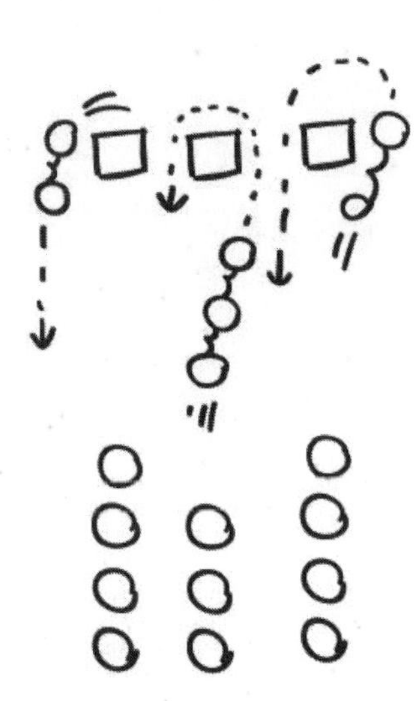

YOU WILL NEED

4 markers (could be a chair or leader)

FORMATION

Four equal teams with the smallest in the front, tallest at the back (about 10 in a team). Each team spaced about four metres from other teams.

HOW TO PLAY

At the word 'go' the first player runs round the marker and back to the front of the team where he takes the hand of the next person, so that the two of them run round hand in hand, come back and collect the next person until the entire team is joined up and has run round the marker and back in line.

It is important that the youngest leads each round as the ones at the end have to run at high speed.

Players running must not break the chain.

WINNER

The first team to be back where they started from.

VARIATION

Instead of one marker for each team, have just the one shared marker for two teams to go round (for 4 teams you will need 2 markers)!

LEARNING POINTS

- Keeping hold of another's hand is difficult. Sometimes you will let go even if you do not intend to. There is only person who never lets us go.
- We may be a 'leader' or a 'follower' but we need to be sure who we are following or where we are lead in life.

Right Order

(an Icebreaker)

space	large
age	11 to 18
number	10 to 30
time	5 to 15 minutes
leaders	2

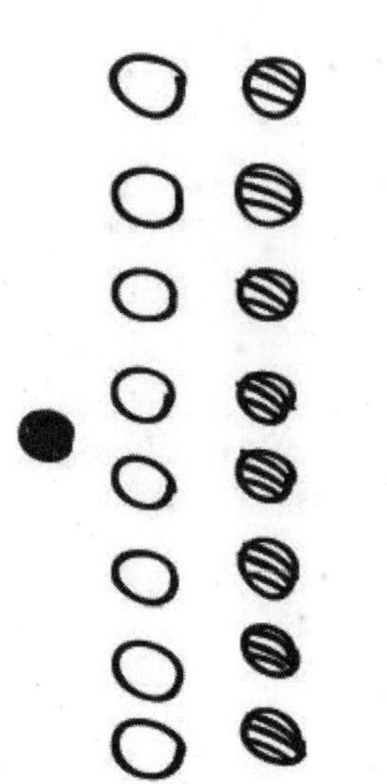

YOU WILL NEED

Nothing.

FORMATION

Everyone in equal teams and straight lines about a metre from the other teams.

HOW TO PLAY

Tell the teams that they need to arrange themselves into the correct alphabetical order in terms of first names. In other words, John, Andrew, Peter etc. should move to an order of Andrew, John, Peter etc. When the team has done this they should sit down.

WINNER

The first team with everyone in the right order. The leader should check!

VARIATION

You can use the month of birth or the family name etc.

The players can be standing on chairs and have to change places without stepping off the chairs.

LEARNING POINT

Getting to know each other is important.

Story Relay

(a Bible game)

space	large
age	5 to 11
number	12 to 30
time	5 to 10 mins
leaders	2

YOU WILL NEED

One chair or marker for each team.

FORMATION

Equal teams sitting in straight lines facing forward with the smallest at the front.

HOW TO PLAY

Tell the story with children representing names or things in the story. For example, the story of Jonah. Young people in teams named as: Jonah / Captain / Sea / Nineveh / Crew / Whale / Fear / People etc.

When they hear 'their' word they run round a chair at the front and go back to their seat. Someone to keep score as the game progresses.

Half way through you can stop the game and tell them you want to finish the story without them running, because it is so exciting.

Don't forget to make the application point!

WINNER

Is the team with the highest score.

LEARNING POINT

As with Jonah: even if we disobey God he still loves us and wants us to do his will.

Team Catch

space	medium
age	5 to 10
number	40
time	5 minutes
leaders	3

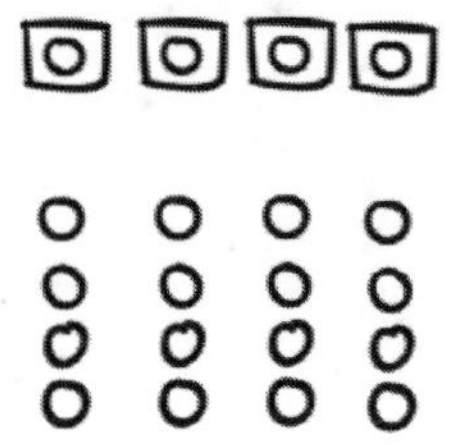

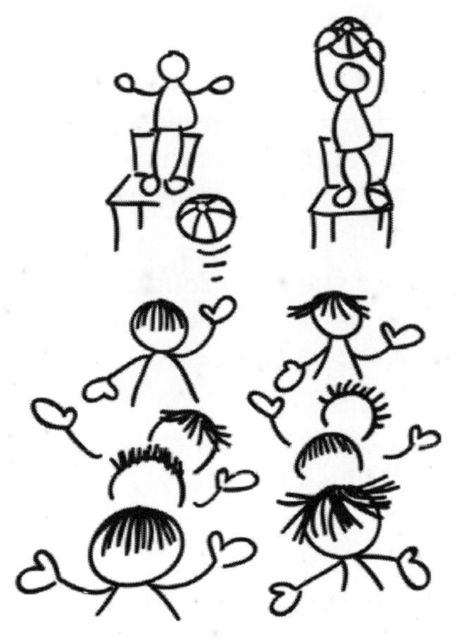

YOU WILL NEED

- 4 large balls
- 4 chairs
- leaders to score

FORMATION

In four equal teams facing a chair two metres from the front of each team.

HOW TO PLAY

First person stands on their chair facing their team. The next in line throws the ball so that the person on the chair can catch it.

If the ball is caught the catcher jumps down and runs to the back of their team. While the thrower goes to stand on the chair for their turn, the ball is passed from the back of the team to the front and the process is repeated. If the catcher does not catch the ball they come down anyway, retrieve the ball and run to the back of the team. 5 points for each catch and 10 for the first team to finish.

WINNER

Is the team with the highest score.

Telephone Chain

(also known as Whispers)

space	medium
age	8 to 18
number	12 to 30
time	5 minutes
leaders	1 per team

YOU WILL NEED

A short message — the same for each team.

FORMATION

Standing or sitting in line in their teams.

HOW TO PLAY

The first child from each team goes to the leader to hear the message, then quickly returns to their team to whisper it to the second child in their team. The second child passes it on by whispering to the third, and so on until the end of the line.

The last child then tells their leader what the message is, so that they can write it down.

WINNER

The winner is the first team to get the 'transmission' correct.

LEARNING POINTS

We often do not communicate things clearly which brings misunderstandings and difficulties. But God gives us His Word, which does not change.

Throw Ball

space	large
age	8 to 14
number	10 to 40
time	5 minutes
leaders	2

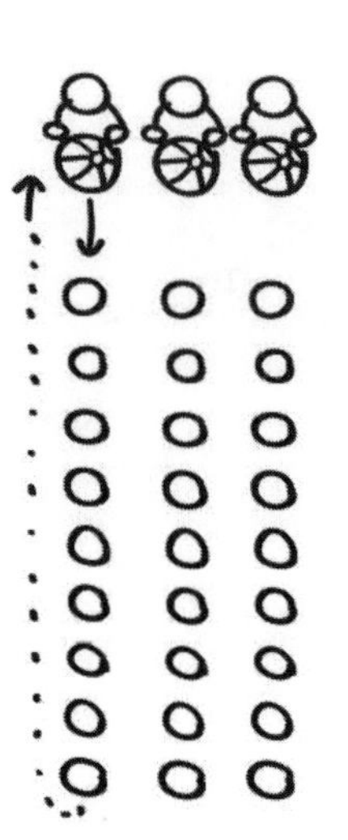

YOU WILL NEED

One ball (large if possible) for each team.

FORMATION

Teams in straight lines, one behind the other. There should be the same number in each team. Up to about 10 in each team.

HOW TO PLAY

The first person in the team comes forward one metre and faces their team. They are given a ball each. At the word 'go' they throw it to the first one in the team, who returns it to the thrower, then crouches down. The thrower sends the ball to the next in the team and so on until the ball arrives at the last person in the team, who DOES NOT THROW IT BACK but runs, with the ball, to take the place of the thrower. The first thrower moves to the FRONT of the team ready to catch the ball from the new thrower, who has just run from the back.

WINNER

The first team to be back where they started from. Extra points for the quietest team in the straightest line.

VARIATION

If you do not have balls you can use bean bags. Could even try balloons filled with water!

LEARNING POINT

In life you will have to do many things which gradually get harder. Practise, don't give up.

Tunnel Ball

space	large
age	8 to 14
number	10 to 40
time	5 minutes
leaders	2

YOU WILL NEED

One ball per team (large if possible).

FORMATION

Teams in straight lines, one behind the other and with their legs apart. There should be the same number in each team. Up to about 10 players in each team.

HOW TO PLAY

The first person in each team is given a ball. At the word 'go' the ball is rolled between their legs so that it will eventually reach the last person who picks it up, runs to the front and repeats the exercise. The game continues until everyone is back at their starting point.

WINNER

The first team to be back where they started from, sitting quietly!

Under Over

space	large
age	8 to 14
number	10 to 40
time	5 minutes
leaders	2

YOU WILL NEED

One ball per team.

FORMATION

Teams in straight lines, one behind the other. There should be the same number of children in each team.

HOW TO PLAY

The first child in each team is given a ball. At the word, 'Go!' the child passes the ball backwards, over his head to the child behind. This child passes the ball backwards between his legs, to the child behind, who then passes the pall over his head, in the same fashion as the first, and so on. When the ball reaches the last child, he runs with the ball to the front and the process is repeated until everyone is back in their starting place.

WINNER

Is the first team sitting quietly back in their starting place.

LEARNING POINT

Just as there are ups and downs with the path of the ball, our lives have ups and downs too. So it is good to have Jesus with us on the way.

Water Relay

space	large
age	8 to 18
number	10 to 30
time	10 minutes
leaders	2 or 3

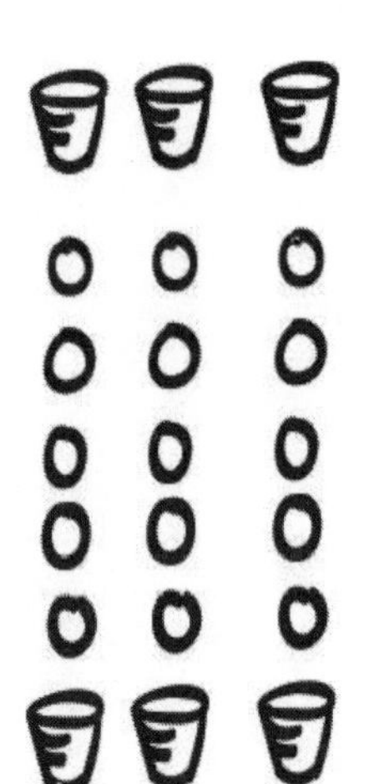

YOU WILL NEED

- 2 buckets for each team
- 3 cups or bowls (plastic — not glass) for each team
- water

FORMATION

Standing one behind another in teams.

HOW TO PLAY

Each team has a bucket filled with water at the front of the team with three cups or bowls nearby. There is an empty bucket two metres behind them. The first in line fills the cup or bowl with water and, while still facing the front, pass it over their head with BOTH HANDS to the person behind and so on. The last in line empties the water into the bucket behind, then runs round to the front to fill the cup up with water and repeat. You can have two or three cups being passed down the line at once. Stop when the front bucket is empty or the other bucket full!

WINNER

The team with the most water in their bucket.

VARIATION

Each team chooses one member to carry the water in the bucket to the other bucket whilst being carried by the other team members over obstacles.

Put a small hole in the bottom of the cup!

Two Teams

These games involve two teams only playing in opposition against each other, with the leader keeping the score. In some Two Team games, not all the players play at once. Only one or two from each team play at a time.

Balloon Smash

space	medium
age	8 to 11
number	10 to 20
time	10 minutes
leaders	1

YOU WILL NEED

4 or 5 balloons

FORMATION

The two teams sit back to back on chairs

HOW TO PLAY

To begin, the leader throws a balloon in over the heads of the seated players.

The task is for each team to try to hit the balloon backwards over their heads and those of the other team so that the balloon lands on the floor out of their reach. They have to do this while remaining seated all the time.

If they manage to achieve this, they score one point for their team and the balloon is put into play again. More than one balloon can be used at a time.

If a balloon comes out at the side a leader may put it back into play.

WINNER

Is the team with the highest score.

LEARNING POINT

The Christian life is not always easy and you need to work as a team.

Bash Away

space	medium
age	8 to 14
number	10 to 30
time	5 to 10 minutes
leaders	1

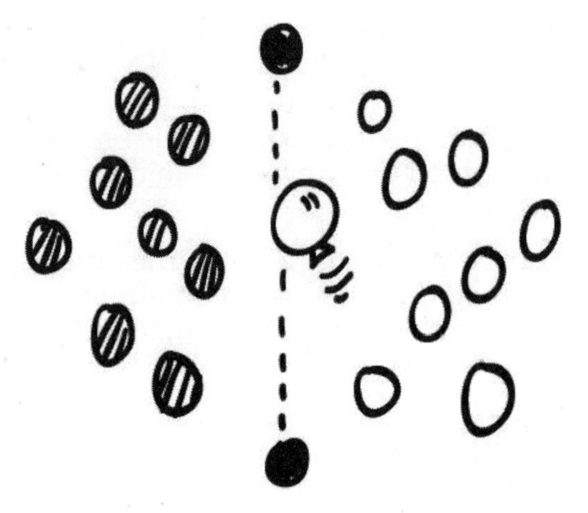

YOU WILL NEED

5 balloons

FORMATION

Two teams facing each other in different halves of playing area which is roughly divided into two.

HOW TO PLAY

One or two balloons are put into the central area and the teams have to get them out of their area while the leader counts up to 10 or 15 and shouts 'stop' or blows a whistle. (The leader should not be looking at the play, otherwise she or he might give advantage to one side.) The team without the balloon in their area gains a point. Nobody should touch the balloon after the leader signals to stop.

It is probably good to put the balloons (if more than one is used) at the back of each group when you start.

Nobody must go out of their area.

WINNER

Is the team with the highest score.

VARIATION

Throw in 5 balloons and when the time is up count how many balloons are in each place.

If you have four teams divide the playing area into four with one team in each quarter. Like this the balloons can come from any direction. Once again the play must stop when the leader says so.

LEARNING POINT

Keep bad things out of your life.

Binball

(like 'Ringer')

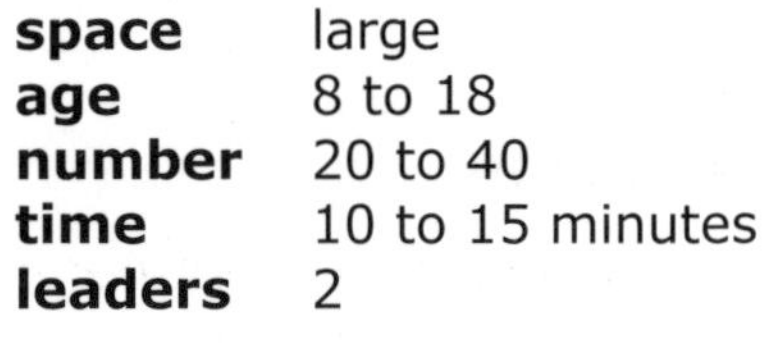

space large
age 8 to 18
number 20 to 40
time 10 to 15 minutes
leaders 2

chair
or box

chair
or box

YOU WILL NEED

- 2 chairs
- two baskets or buckets or bins
- a large ball

FORMATION

Two teams on different ends of the playing area. One team member stands with a bin on a chair at the opposite end to the team.

HOW TO PLAY

The aim of the game is for the ball to be dropped or thrown into the basket or bucket and not fall out. The team players can move anywhere but cannot move if they have possession of the ball. Each team tries to score by getting the ball into their bin, while preventing the other side from scoring.

RULES

- No running while carrying the ball.
- No snatching the ball from another child.
- The ball must not be placed in the bin.
- The person on the chair or box must not fall off.
- If a defender touches the person on the chair there will be a penalty shot from four metres for the other team.

WINNER

The winner is the team with the highest score at the end of the game, which should last about ten minutes.

VARIATION

If bigger children, or boys in a mixed group, dominate the game, get them to sit out while the others play until a goal is scored, then swap players over.

LEARNING POINT

You cannot do it alone.

Cap Snatch

space	medium
age	8 or above
number	10 to 20
time	10 minutes
leaders	2

YOU WILL NEED

A cap or cloth

FORMATION

Divide into two teams of equal numbers standing in straight lines. Number them off 1, 2, 3, etc.

HOW TO PLAY

Each child partners with their opposite number in the other team. When the leader calls a number, players with that number rush towards the cap and try to bring it back to their line <u>without being touched</u> by the other player. The player who succeeds earns one point for the team.

However, if the player is touched by the opponent while holding the cap, the point is lost to the other team.

Players return to their place in the line and another number is called.

WINNER

Is the team to get 10 points first.

LEARNING POINT

There is a time to wait and a time to act.

Chair Balloon Bash

(similar idea to table football)

space	large
age	8 to 18
number	40
time	10 minutes
leaders	4

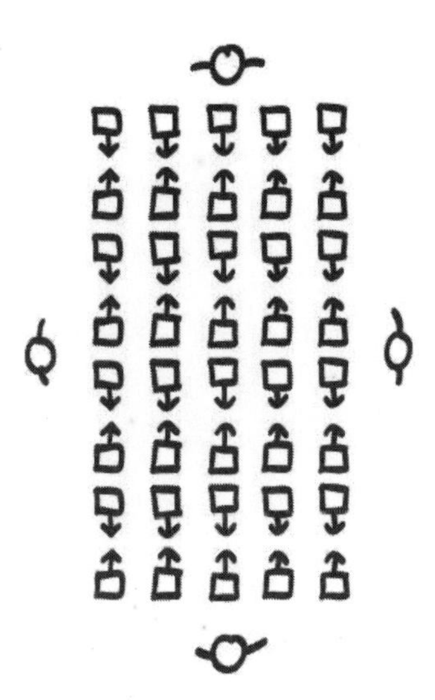

YOU WILL NEED

- one chair for each child
- one or two large balloons

FORMATION

Rows of chairs as per the picture for the number of children playing, maximum 40. Chairs will be back to back and one metre between the facing chairs in front and those on either side.

HOW TO PLAY

There are two teams. One team face one way, the second team the other way. A large balloon is dropped into the playing area and the children have to pat it in the direction they are facing with the objective of getting it over the defenders rows to their team players in front of them and ultimately over the final row of defenders.

If a child raises themselves off their chair they have to spend 10 seconds in the penalty zone (a chair outside the playing area).

When a point is scored the balloon is put in the centre again.

Leaders need to be stationed at the sides to keep the balloon in play.

WINNER

A goal is scored if the balloon touches the ground behind the defenders. Winner is the team with the highest score.

VARIATION

When they get used to this game complicate it by having a second balloon in play.

LEARNING POINT

You cannot win as a Christian on your own. We are part of a body and need each other in order to succeed.

Crocker

(similar to baseball)

space	large
age	8 to 18 years
number	20 to 50 players
time	30 minutes
leaders	3

YOU WILL NEED

- large soft ball and 2 or 4 paper batons.
- 3 chairs or similar size objects.
- a leader to keep score in each team.

HOW TO PLAY

There are two teams. One team (the 'batters') has to score points by hitting the ball, thrown from four metres away, with a stick or baton. The batters are to line up along the wall near to the chair. If the batter touches the ball in any way with the stick or bat, he has to run round the marker four metres away and back to defend the chair again ready for the next throw. If the 'bowler' (the person on the other team to deliver the ball to the batters) hits the back or seat of the chair with the ball, then the batter is out and the next player quickly takes his turn to try to score. There is a continuous attack on the chair whether the batter is there or not. The bowler can get the batter 'out' even if when the batter is going round the marker. The batter can also be out if the ball is caught, after being hit.

The other team (the 'fielders') are there to get the batting team out and they have to spread themselves about to catch the ball and to get the ball back to the bowler. The bowler must throw the ball underarm to aim to hit the chair seat or back — but not the chair legs. The ball must not bounce before it reaches the chair. The team must work quickly in their task to get the team out. When the first team has all had one turn to bat the teams change places and the new batting team will try to beat the other's score.

WINNER

Is the team with the highest score.

LEARNING POINT

Everyone has their part to play and is important.

Guess What?

space small
age 8 to 18
number 30
time 10 minutes
leaders 1

YOU WILL NEED

- the liquid mix:e.g. coke, orange juice, a little vinegar, pepper, salt, tomato ketchup, and a clean sock in a pot.
- a table
- an empty glass
- spoons

FORMATION

In teams (circles or lines). Place the pot on the table and the empty glass beside it.

HOW TO PLAY

Tell the children that this is a competition to work out the recipe of the drink in the pot at the front. The group who is best at tasting will work out the ingredients.

Pour some liquid from the pot into the glass. Invite one person from each team to come up and have a sip from a spoon. When they have tasted they return to their team and others take turns to taste it.

Each team tries to make a list of what is in the drink. At the close ask them what they think was in the drink.

When you have checked the list and pronounced the winner say: 'I will just have a look in the pot in case I have forgotten anything'. You can add: 'you know I have been getting a little forgetful lately, I even came out today without my sock on'. Pull your trouser leg up and show a bare foot. 'Now I wonder where I put it'. Go to the pot and pull out the sock! Then run!

WINNER

Is the group who guessed the most ingredients.

LEARNING POINT

You cannot trust everybody in life. Test what is really true.

Hit the Bottle

space large
age 8 or above
number 10 to 40
time 10 to 20 minutes
leaders 3

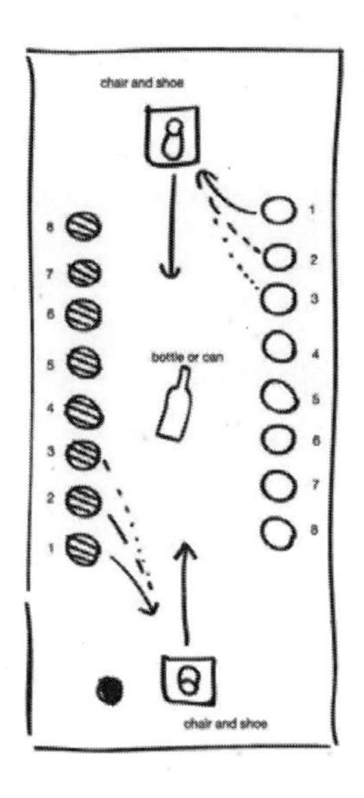

YOU WILL NEED

- 2 chairs or boxes
- plastic bottle or can.
- 2 bean bags or balls (to throw)

FORMATION

Two teams — each team shoulder to shoulder in height order — each team to face each other at opposite ends to opponent, as per diagram.

HOW TO PLAY

Each team to be numbered (smallest to be first). Leader calls a number and that child runs to the chair TO THEIR RIGHT. They pick up the ball or beanbag, then they stand on the chair and throw the ball or beanbag to try to hit the empty bottle or can situated halfway between the chairs. If they miss they run, pick up their ball or beanbag and climb on the opposite chair and try again. Both keep trying until one of them knocks the bottle over, scoring a point for their team. They return the ball or beanbag to their chair and go back to their place in the team and the leader calls another number.

(A point can be taken off their score if they don't return the ball or beanbag to their chair!)

WINNER

The team with the most points at the end.

VARIATION

As a surprise, ask a leader to move the chairs to a more distant place to make it more challenging for older children. If children miss twice bring both chairs in one metre at a time.

Bring the chairs much closer for small children.

Hit the Tin

(similar to unihoc or hockey)

space	large
age	8 to 18 years
number	16 to 30 players
time	10 minutes
leaders	2

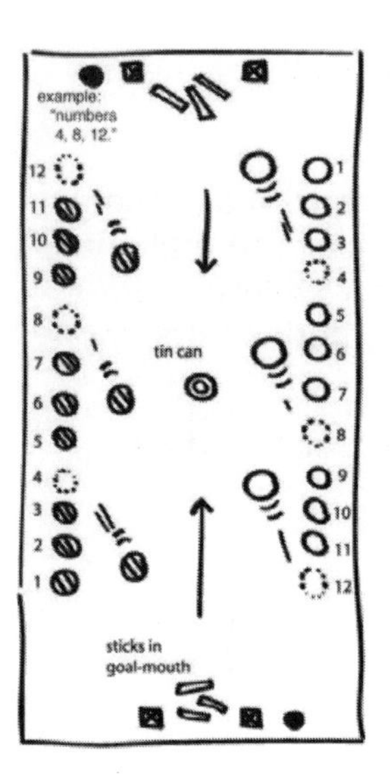

YOU WILL NEED

- 4 or 6 paper sticks (rolled up newspaper well taped)
- 2 goal areas marked 4 metres wide
- old tin can
- (paper and pencil to write down the numbers in the teams)

HOW TO PLAY

Begin with both teams facing each other and numbered in height order as shown in the drawing.

The leader calls two or three numbers. The people with those numbers in each team, run to the goal to their right; pick up the 'sticks' from their goalmouth and try to hit the can into the opposite goal, as in hockey. When someone scores the players return to their teams and the leader calls out two more numbers. Someone keeps score.

WINNER

Is the team with the highest score after everyone has had a turn.

VARIATION

Change the size of the goal area. If you want a fast game then make it very wide.

Kabadi

space	large
age	8 to 18
number	12
time	10 minutes
leaders	2

YOU WILL NEED

- a marked area
- a good referee

FORMATION

This is probably the most popular game in India and is great fun.

You need a rectangle marked out approximately 5 by 10 metres but the size can vary. If you have more people in the team, make the play area bigger. The area is divided in half to make approximately two areas of 5 X 5 — one for each team.

HOW TO PLAY

The teams decide for who starts. The team starting, 'A' team, chooses one person to open the contest. That person takes a deep breath because when he enters team B's area he may not take a breath and has to keep saying 'Kabadi, kabadi, kabadi…' out loud continuously so the others will know he has not taken a breath. While in 'B' team's area his task is to touch one person and then to make a dash back to his own side without being caught. The person touched is then eliminated from his team and leaves the playing area. BUT if the B team can surround him and prevent his return or he takes a breath he is eliminated and he leaves the play area. So the teams get smaller and smaller until there is a winner.

Everyone has to take a turn to go into the opponent's side.

WINNER

Is the team which survives.

LEARNING POINT

We need to take risks sometimes, but be careful that nothing can catch us out.

Ladder Balloons

space	medium
age	8 to 14
number	16 to 20
time	10 minutes
leaders	1

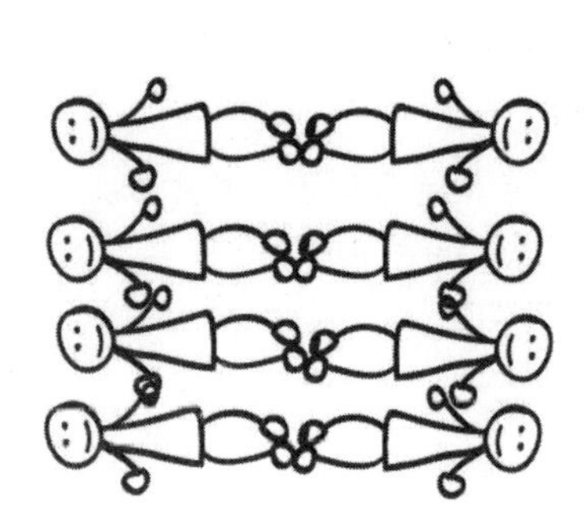

YOU WILL NEED

Balloons

FORMATION

The Group is divided into two teams. They lie down with their feet against the feet of their opponent in the other team, like the rungs of a ladder.

HOW TO PLAY

Using a balloon, they play 'volleyball' with their hands. To score, they must hit the balloon to land on the floor behind the other team. They are not allowed to lift their legs or feet or sit up. The leader counts the points when the balloon goes out. After a while, add more balloons.

WINNER

Is the team with the highest score.

VARIATION

In hot weather, you could put a little water into the balloons first.

LEARNING POINT

Be ready at all times.

Not Funny

space	medium
age	5 to 14
number	12 to 40
time	5 to 10 minutes
leaders	1

YOU WILL NEED

Nothing

HOW TO PLAY

Team A must make Team B laugh in less than one minute, by making faces, laughing, etc. No touching is allowed. Then Team B must make team A laugh. The leader should time how long it takes for the team to be out.

WINNER

Is the team which can be serious the longest.

VARIATION

Statues (see All Together)

Noughts 'n' Crosses

space	medium
age	6 to 18
number	20
time	8 minutes
leaders	2

YOU WILL NEED

9 chairs

FORMATION

One team is at one end of the hall and the other team facing them at the other end. One team are 0's and the other are X's. In between each team are 9 chairs, which are placed so you have three lines of three, spaced half a metre between each other.

HOW TO PLAY

When the whistle is blown one person from each team runs to a chair and sits down. At the next whistle two others (one from each team) run and sit down. Continue like this until one team has three of their players in a straight or diagonal row. Have three rounds to determine a winner.

The first person to touch a chair gets to sit on it, no pushing.

WINNER

Is the team with the highest score.

VARIATION

With larger numbers of children, make extra teams. You can have the two winning teams playing each other to find the champion team. And the two losing teams can have a play off to see who comes third.

LEARNING POINT

Be careful where you choose to be in life. It's easy to go to the wrong place with the wrong people.

Paper Fight

space	medium
age	8 to 18
number	20
time	5 minutes
leaders	2

YOU WILL NEED

- chairs for each team
- 3 or 4 sheets of newspaper per child
- 2 paper hats or some item to put on the target's head
- very strict and careful judging

FORMATION

Two teams seated on chairs facing each other in straight lines about a metre apart. One person from each team has to sit behind their team with a paper hat on their heads (or something loose fitting but the same for both teams). All the other team members are given between two and four sheets of newspaper.

HOW TO PLAY

When the game starts the children with the paper tear it up to make paper balls to throw over their opponents at the enemy's hat. One hit is 5 points and if the hat is knocked off 10 points are scored. A leader needs to be beside each target person to put the hat back on as soon as it is knocked off. Players must not leave their seats, or else a penalty is incurred and 5 points are given to the other team.

WINNER

Is the team with the highest score after a given period of time.

Ringer

(in the style of Binball)

space	large
age	8 to 18
number	10 to 40
time	15 to 30 minutes
leaders	3

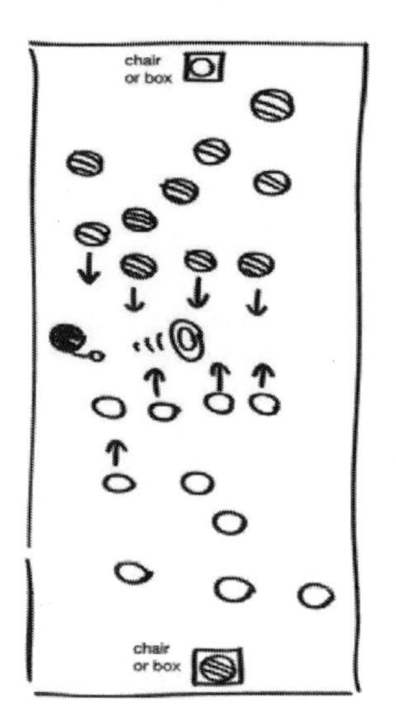

YOU WILL NEED

- 2 chairs or boxes
- 2 sticks of rolled up newspaper
- a ring of rubber, rope or paper

FORMATION

Two teams, one at each end of the playing area. Each team has one team member stands on the chair at the opposite end holding a rolled up paper stick.

HOW TO PLAY

When the game starts the RING is thrown into the area. Each team must prevent the other team scoring, while they try to pass the ring from one to another until it can be thrown over the rolled-up newspaper held by their player at the other end of the playing area. There is no limit to the play area, you can play behind the chairs, anywhere! Strict refereeing is essential.

RULES

- No running when holding the ring.
- No pulling the ring from another's hand.
- The ring must not be PLACED on the stick (roll). It must be thrown.
- No touching the person on the chair.

WINNER

The winner is the team with the highest score after a given time.

VARIATION

If bigger children dominate the game, have them sit out after a goal is scored, and the little ones play until they score a goal - or the boys sit out so that the girls have a chance.

Round The Circle

space large
age 8 to 14
number 10 to 20
time 15 minutes
leaders 2

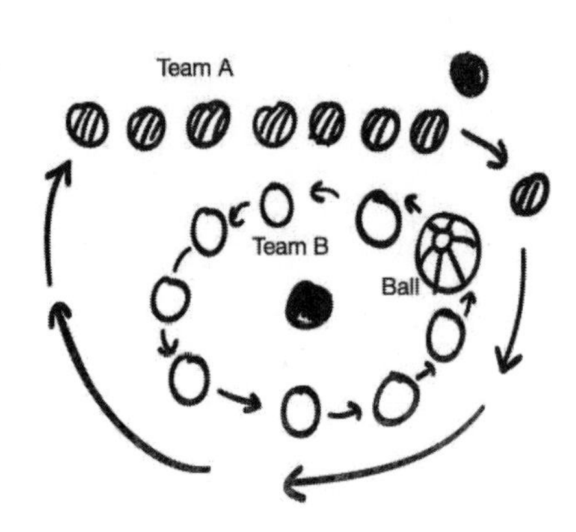

YOU WILL NEED

- a baton
- a large ball

FORMATION

Team 'A' in a straight line, with the baton. Team 'B' with ball, in a circle close to each other.

HOW TO PLAY

Both teams start at the same time. The front person in team 'A' runs round circle 'B', to the back of his team with the baton, which is then passed down from person to person to the child at the front, who then runs round circle 'B' etc. When all have been round they shout, 'STOP'. In the meantime, team 'B' throw the ball round their circle counting aloud each time someone catches. (Has to be thrown not passed).

The object for team 'B' is to see how many times they can pass the ball before team 'A' shout 'stop'. Their score is recorded and the teams swap their formation with 'A' making a circle and 'B' the straight line.

WINNER

Is the team with the highest number of passes.

VARIATION

Let a leader stand in the centre of the circle with the ball being thrown between the leader and the players in the circle instead of the ball just going round the circle.

LEARNING POINT

It is good to have an aim in life — a target to reach.

Snakes Tail

space	large
age	11 to 18
number	10 to 40
time	10 minutes
leaders	2

YOU WILL NEED

1 strip of cloth 50 cm long for each team.

FORMATION

Each team has the youngest or shortest person at the front and the tallest at the back. Each team member holds the waist of the person in front. It is best to have no more than three teams.

HOW TO PLAY

The last member of each team has a strip of cloth (tail) hanging from the waist band of their trousers. (it should be able to be pulled off easily). The task for each snake is to prevent their tail from being taken, while the person at the head of the snake must try to snatch the tail from their opponents! So the snake has to both attack and defend. If the head of the snake moves too quickly the chain may be broken and a point will go to the other side.

WINNER

Is the snake which either gets the tail off the other team first

OR

scores because the other team breaks in two!

OR

is the snake which does not lose its tail!

LEARNING POINT

The Christian life involves both going forward as well as defending yourself so you do not get dragged into bad ways.

Snatch It

space	medium
age	8 to 18
number	10 to 30
time	10 minutes
leaders	2

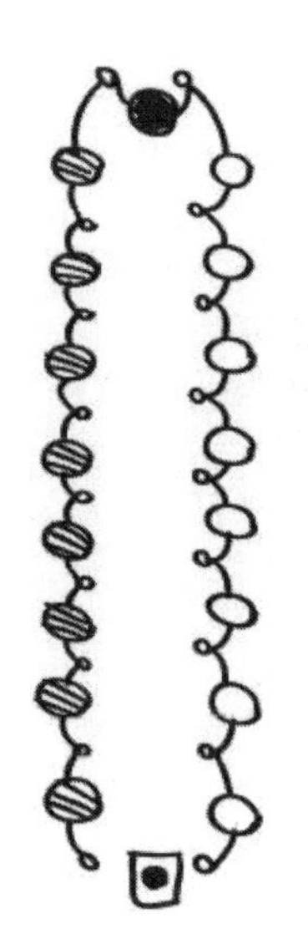

YOU WILL NEED

- a small item
- a chair or table

FORMATION

Two teams in straight lines, facing each other about one metre apart. Put a chair at one end between them, with the item on it and equal distance from the teams.

HOW TO PLAY

Each team has to hold hands. The leader holds the hands of the two at the front of the teams. When the leader secretly squeezes the hands of the first two they are, in turn, to pass the 'squeeze' down the line. When the end person has their hand squeezed they are to grab the item on the chair with their free hand before the other person does.

After each turn, the one at the front of each team goes to the back.

WINNER

The first person to get the item. A score should be kept. If someone grabs the item before the leader squeezes the hands then a point is deducted from the team.

VARIATION

The leader can pretend to squeeze but, in fact, does not.

The leader can also place both his hands and those of the first two in the team behind his back so there is no chance of anyone in the line seeing the first 'squeeze'.

Sound Barrier

space medium
age 8 to 15
number 16 to 24
time 10 minutes
leaders 1

YOU WILL NEED

Nothing.

FORMATION

Divide the players into two teams, A and B. Team B stands in a line between two halves of team A.

HOW TO PLAY

Half of team A secretly decide on a sentence that they want to communicate to the other half of their team on the other side of team B. At the leader's signal, team A shouts the sentence as loudly as possible to their team mates, while team B tries to put them off and hinder the message (also by shouting). The other half of team A have to try and work out what the message is. When they succeed, put team A in the middle and split team B to do the message. The leader must time the event.

WINNER

The team who gets their message across in the shortest time.

LEARNING POINT

God wants to tell us many important things. Who is hindering us from hearing?

Waterballoon

space large
age 8 to 18
number 4 or more
time 5 minutes
leaders 1

YOU WILL NEED

2 or more water filled balloons for each pair.

FORMATION

In pairs, 2 from each team standing one metre from partner facing each other.

HOW TO PLAY

Everyone will enjoy this. Have everyone divided into teams. Each team must select two people to see how far they can throw a balloon. DO NOT TELL THEM IT IS A WATER FILLED BALLOON. You now have 4+ players in the centre of the group. (The balloons are now brought out and given to the players).

They have to stand one metre from each other and have to gently throw the balloon from one to the other and back again. Every time they successfully catch the balloon they take a step BACK and so on.

The pair which throw the furthest earn a point for their team. These players then return to their place, and the leader calls out two more players from each team.

WINNER

The team with the highest score.

LEARNING POINTS

In life sometimes you have to take risks. It is the same with faith.

Water Volleyballoon

space	large
age	8 or above
number	12 to 30
time	10 minutes
leaders	2

YOU WILL NEED

Water–filled balloons

2 old sheets or curtains. The sheet can be one and a half metres square.

FORMATION

4 teams; 2 teams stand in a straight line side by side to form the 'net', the other teams stand one either side with a sheet each.

HOW TO PLAY

Place a balloon into one of the sheets. Explain: the team has to eject the balloon from the sheet, over the 'net' and the team on the other side have to catch it in their sheet.

If they catch it, they score a point; if not and the balloon bursts, the other team score. They take turns to eject the balloon.

Halfway through, the teams change over. The teams forming the 'net' try scoring with the balloons and the others become the 'net'.

WINNER

Is the team with the highest score.

VARIATION

The winning teams from the first and second half have a play off.

Then take the sheets or curtains away and just throw the balloons over the net by hand and attempts to catch it by hand. The main objective here is that people get wet, especially the leaders.